STARS!

Daphne Davis

STARS!

A FIRESIDE BOOK
Published by Simon & Schuster, Inc.
New York

Designer   Nai Chang
Editor   Marya Dalrymple
Photo research   Daphne Davis

Page 1: Charlie Chaplin in *Modern Times*.
Page 2: Meryl Streep, photograph by Frederic Ohringer.
Page 3: Barbra Streisand in *A Star Is Born*.
Page 4: Faye Dunaway and Warren Beatty in *Bonnie and Clyde*.
Page 5: Humphrey Bogart and Mary Astor in *Across the Pacific*.
Page 6: John Travolta and Karen Lynn Gorney in *Saturday Night Fever*.
Page 7: Fred Astaire in *Blue Skies*.
Pages 8-9: Spencer Tracy and Katharine Hepburn in *Woman of the Year*.
Page 10: Dustin Hoffman in *Tootsie*.
Page 11: Gloria Swanson in *Sunset Boulevard*.
Page 12: Mae West in *Belle of the Nineties*.

Library of Congress Cataloging in Publication Data

Davis, Daphne
    Stars!

Bibliography: p. 272
Includes index.
    1. Moving-picture actors and actresses—United States—Portraits.   2. Moving-picture actors and actresses—United States—Biography.   I. Title
PN1998.A2D38   1984   791.43'028'0922
[B]   84-13897   ISBN 0-671-53083-6

A Fireside Book. Published by Simon & Schuster, Inc., Simon & Schuster Building, Rockefeller Center, 1230 Avenue of the Americas, New York, New York 10020

FIRESIDE and colophon are registered trademarks of Simon & Schuster, Inc.

ISBN: 0-671-53083-6

Printed and bound in Japan

Contents

Introduction

"An idea, in the highest sense of that word, cannot be conveyed but by a symbol."
—Samuel Taylor Coleridge

If, as film historians agree, it was the public that created the movie star system, then it was also the public that dictated which images of movie stars it would accept and worship, thus perpetuating the notion of *star quality*. We are fascinated by certain stars and read about the details of their films and lives not only for what this information tells us about the good and bad attributes of a favorite film actor or actress but also for what the data confirms or denies about ourselves.

What the public has chosen to preserve, cherish, and retain of almost eighty years of movie star photography is collected in *STARS!*, an album of treasured on- and off-screen images of nearly fifty of the most enduring film superstars from 1910 to the present. These illustrations encompass movie stills and publicity head shots, famous and historical portraits and photographic essays, reportorial pictures, and artifacts that are the public's own interpretation of certain superstars —the W. C. Fields cocktail napkin, the Warren Beatty dollar bill, the John Wayne Great American button.

If, in specific instances, movie star photography succeeds as deliberate or serious art, it is largely accident and not design because the subject matter, by nature, is uncontrollable and ephemeral. Long after we have been overwhelmed by the physicality of film actors and actresses, we remain their supporters or detractors on the basis of their staying power and their natural identities, gestures, and character traits—which a photographer's camera can neither force out nor cover up. Captured in a movie still or a newspaper photograph, a star's image symbolizes what he or she is forever and not what the star might be or should have been.

Admired for being unpretentious and slick at the same time, the movie actors and actresses who are described in this book represent a mating of contradictions and share (whether it is true or not) a type of accidentally-on-purpose fame, which is interpreted and reinforced through photographs. Whereas Charlie Chaplin was perceived as poor and good in movies but rich and bad in life, Marlon Brando is consistently viewed as a nonconformist in his words and actions.

In portraits of the kings and queens of the silent era, Victorian *tableau vivant* photography focused on the star in costume (Mary Pickford's little girl, Rudolf Valentino's sheik). The star *was* the costume and the costume *was* the star's identity no matter what he or she did or said on or off camera.

The development in the 1920s of Panchromatic film enabled movie cameras to reproduce on screen the perfection of fashion magazine close-ups. Greta Garbo's haunting face became synonymous with the close-up. Likewise, the technical advances in full figure movement photography of the Fred Astaire-Ginger Rogers dance musicals helped to define the pace and scale of action in comedies and westerns.

In the 1930s and 1940s, candid head shots and medium-shot confrontational photography promoted the personality traits of movie stars: the upward mobility of Joan Crawford's working girls, the theatrical mannerisms of Bette Davis, the amicable battle of the sexes between Katharine Hepburn and Spencer Tracy, and the disillusionment of Humphrey Bogart's tough guy. In the 1950s, James Dean's rebels would add raw emotions to the process.

But it is narcissism that has always been the lifeblood of movie star photography. Nude movie star centerfold photographs, like those of sex symbol Marilyn Monroe and playboy Burt Reynolds, homogenized comparison (How does what I have compare to what he or she has?) photography and occasionally stretched it to the level of an art form. With the blurring of paparazzi and television news photography in the 1960s and 1970s, movie star photographers strived to capture both the ideal and real sides of movie heroes and heroines: love goddess Elizabeth Taylor's endless illnesses and marriages and divorces; Barbra Streisand's superstar-ness; Robert Redford's winner persona; and Jane Fonda's protests.

In the 1970s, the medium was infiltrated by the photographically clinical aspects of soft and hard core pornography (pretty baby Brooke Shields and pretty boy John Travolta). And in the 1980s, movie megastars like maverick Harrison Ford and outerspace creatures like E.T. The Extra-Terrestrial are captured in mind-altering, special effects photography.

Finally, in movie star photography—so similar to platitudes and clichés—every picture tells a story by establishing and resolving a moral, fable, or parody of cinematic hope and despair. On the occasions when the images and styles of movie star photographs have been compared to and considered great art, it is because they crystallize truth through illusion. As writer Roland Barthes noted, a photograph is the idea of reality that permits us to live in our imagination.

—DAPHNE DAVIS

Faye Dunaway, as Joan Crawford in *Mommie Dearest*, poses for George Hurrell, as they recreate his photograph of Crawford.

The Kings and Queens of the Silver Screen

Mary Pickford
America's Sweetheart

Real name: Gladys Marie Smith; Born: April 9, 1893; Died: May 29, 1979
*Academy Awards: Best Actress, Coquette; Special Oscar "in recognition of her unique contributions
to the film industry and the development of film as an artistic medium."*

She was the birth and death of innocence in American movies. As the country went from rural to urban, and values switched from moral to monetary, Mary Pickford exemplified the American Dream—the person who rose by talent from rags to great wealth. What better way to exhibit the rewards of the dream than to be a child forever. And what better person to re-create the illusion of childhood than a girl who never had one.

After her father's death, Baby Gladys Smith became, at five, the family breadwinner on the stage. Rechristened Mary Pickford in the movies, the dimpled pixie achieved celluloid immortality by playing an adorable child-woman until she was middle-aged. But not all of her sweetheart roles were sickeningly sweet Pollyannas; many were ingenuous little adults who took hold of situations and charged off to find solutions to problems.

Upon scrutiny, Pickford's comedies and dramas are now classified by film historians as class struggles, with "our Mary" championing the poor and deriding the rich. Nevertheless, the premier victim of Hollywood typecasting beat the system—first by forming United Artists with D.W. Griffith, Charlie Chaplin, and husband Douglas Fairbanks (prompting the remark, "The lunatics have taken over the asylum.") and second by amassing a $50 million fortune in real estate.

When America's Sweetheart married all-American swashbuckler Douglas Fairbanks, they invented Hollywood royalty. But the dream spoiled when they divorced and Pickford married Buddy Rogers, her co-star in *My Best Girl*. "I left the screen," she said, "because I didn't want what happened to Charlie Chaplin to happen to me. When he discarded the Little Tramp, the Little Tramp turned around and killed him. The little girl made me. I wasn't waiting for the little girl to kill me." One biographer reports that Pickford, in old age, became a recluse, turning to the Bible and booze, crying out for her mother and true love Douglas Fairbanks, and regaling friends with accounts of the early days of movies.

BELOW: In her thirties, little Mary cut her golden locks. "It was my final revolt against the type of role I had been playing," she recalled in her autobiography. The curls now reside in museums in San Diego and Los Angeles.

OPPOSITE: In Mary Janes, anklets, and frilly frock, Mary Pickford delights as the perpetual imp.

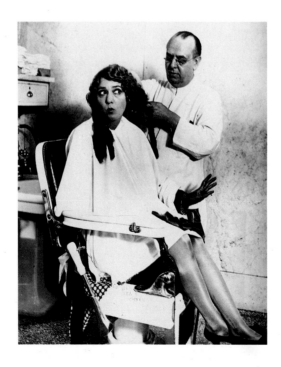

Sincerely
Mary Pickford

ABOVE LEFT: *Rebecca of Sunnybrook Farm* finds the mischievous Mary pilfering a piece of pie after consulting conflicting samplers, one with the motto "Thou shalt not steal" and the other "The Lord helps those who help themselves."

ABOVE CENTER: In *Sparrows*, as clever teenager Momma Molly, Pickford frees orphans from a kidnapping ring.

ABOVE RIGHT: In her last film, *Secrets*, Mary eloped with Leslie Howard and headed West in a covered wagon. Her dramatic talents in the film were highly praised, but by this time audiences had tired of her.

RIGHT: Douglas Fairbanks and Mary Pickford co-starred in a disastrous adaptation of Shakespeare's *The Taming of the Shrew*, which had the credit "additional dialogue by Sam Taylor."

OPPOSITE PAGE

TOP: Pickford with her special Oscar and third husband, Buddy Rogers, who gave Mary her first screen kiss in *My Best Girl*. "She was the only woman I ever loved," said Rogers, who pursued her for ten years until she married him.

BOTTOM: Hollywood's first royal couple dwelled at Pickfair, where they entertained authentic and phony dukes and duchesses. After Pickford's death, the mansion was put on the market for $10 million.

For Pickford's 1909–17 films,
see page 270

Stella Maris, 1918
Amarilly of Clothes-Line Alley, 1918
M'Liss, 1918
How Could You, Jean?, 1918
Johanna Enlists, 1918
Captain Kidd, Jr., 1919
Daddy Long-Legs, 1919
The Hoodlum, 1919
The Heart o' the Hills, 1919
Pollyanna, 1920
Suds, 1920
The Love Light, 1921
Through the Back Door, 1921
Little Lord Fauntleroy, 1921
Tess of the Storm Country, 1922
Rosita, 1923
Dorothy Vernon of Haddon Hall, 1924
Little Annie Rooney, 1925
Sparrows, 1926
My Best Girl, 1927
The Gaucho, 1927
Coquette, 1929
The Taming of the Shrew, 1929
Kiki, 1931
Secrets, 1933

Charlie Chaplin
The Little Tramp

Real name: Charles Spencer Chaplin; Born: April 16, 1889; Died: December 25, 1977
Academy Awards: Special Oscars "for versatility and genius in writing, acting, directing, and producing The Circus *,"*
and "for the incalculable effect he has had in making motion pictures the art form of this century"
Best Original Dramatic Score, Limelight

George Bernard Shaw considered Charlie Chaplin "the one genius created by cinema." As the wiry little tramp with funny and mean faces, Chaplin single-handedly transformed motion picture comedy into an art form. As director, producer, writer, and star, he used satire, pathos, and slapstick to lampoon man's greed and inhumanity to man. His displaced person costume of baggy pants, frayed cutaway, undersized derby, mustache, sporty cane, and bubble-toed boots contrasted him with heroines, cops, villains, and kids. Capturing the soul of the underdog, Chaplin's comic tramp was the gag. He got into and out of trouble but retained his dignity and self-respect by overcoming adversity. Audiences everywhere responded to Chaplin's message about poverty, hunger, and homelessness, and they made the movie folk hero into a symbol of hope.

Humiliated by poverty and a Dickensian childhood, Chaplin longed for an ideal world and an ideal woman. Because he never knew the fun of being a teenager and the thrill of first love with a girl his own age, he enacted these scenarios as an adult. The Joan Barry paternity suit, in which he was acquitted, and his marriages and divorces to teenagers were as scandalous as his misunderstood politics, rooted in a distrust of systems. Some historians now maintain that the social and political persecution of Chaplin was an unconscious reaction to his dichotomous image—poor and good in movies, rich and bad in life.

The finest examples of Charlie Chaplin's craft—*The Gold Rush, City Lights,* and *Modern Times*—had a comic mission. "A world in which people cannot laugh isn't worth saving," he protested in an article explaining why he made *The Great Dictator.* Chaplin and his movies grew in stature after he went into self-exile in Switzerland with his last wife, the serene and maternal Oona O'Neill. Before his death, the virtuoso of silent film comedy was vindicated and showered with honors and awards.

BELOW: "I always knew I was a poet," said the handsome pantomimist, who turned his gift for conveying unspoken emotions into comic film art. This portrait displays Chaplin's melancholy and wonder.

OPPOSITE: Part vaudeville clown, outcast philosopher, and natural aristocrat, Chaplin's gentleman tramp perseveres, hoping things will turn out better.

LEFT: Adolf Hitler supposedly patterned his look on Chaplin's. In *The Great Dictator*, the comedian ferociously burlesqued the fascist megalomaniac as both Adenoid Hynkel and a Jewish barber who's mistaken for Hitler.

ABOVE: In *The Gold Rush*, the masterpiece Chaplin wanted to be remembered for, the starving tramp (a gold prospector in the Klondike) boils and eats his shoe. The "spaghetti" laces and "meat" sole were made of licorice.

BELOW: *Modern Times* was Chaplin's parable denouncing the mechanization of man and society. It reflected his dislike of systems that kick small, helpless people around.

For Chaplin's 1914 films, see page 271

In the allegorical *Limelight*, the tramp appears for the last time as Calvero, a washed-up music hall artist who loves a young ballerina (Claire Bloom). He surrenders her to a younger rival, makes a comeback, and dies.

For a boy who grew up in the slums of Victorian London, Chaplin's life ended as a fairy tale. He married his dream princess, Oona O'Neill, when she was eighteen and he was fifty-six; he was knighted by Queen Elizabeth II in 1975; and he lived happily with his family in Switzerland until his death.

From the left: son-in-law Nick Sistovaris, daughters Annie and Josephine, Chaplin, Oona, son Christopher, and daughters Geraldine and Jane.

Gloria Swanson
Movie Queen

Real name: Gloria May Josephine Swanson; Born: March 27, 1899; Died: April 4, 1983

"Is there anyone who can flaunt a superb wardrobe with more dash than Gloria Swanson?" wrote director Marshall Neilan. But it was costume drama showman Cecil B. DeMille who got Swanson to let go in front of the camera in fancy-dress, modern-marriage tear-jerkers. "You're giving me terribly expensive tastes, Mr. DeMille," the first lady of gaudy movie fashions and outlandish screen comebacks swooned to her spiritual mentor. From *Don't Change Your Husband* and *Why Change Your Wife?* through *Male and Female*, the clothes-horse drew legions of women to movie houses to watch her parade in fashion orgies that were more erotic than the films' handsome leading men. As aristocratic English novelist Elinor Glyn proclaimed to Swanson, "People don't care about royalty anymore. They're more interested in queens of the screen, like you, dear."

The movie queen reached the pinnacle of chic with the Marquis de la Falaise de la Coudraye, a docile and impoverished half-French and half-Irish nobleman who became her third husband. The couple stopped traffic at costume balls in Paris, New York, and Hollywood. Their wedding day in Paris, in 1925, was the saddest and happiest of her life. Swanson was pregnant; but fearful of ruining her career, she had an abortion the next day. "Hank," as she called her marquis, later parted from Swanson because of her affair with Joseph P. Kennedy, Sr. The millionaire entrepreneur took over the star's career only to leave her finances in a shambles.

In between retirements and comebacks, Hollywood's first screen queen fared better at radio, Broadway, and television than she did at love and marriage. "I have the worst taste in men," lamented the complex beauty, who craved being overwhelmed by men more than she enjoyed overwhelming them. Never one to be dejected for long, the professional comeback maker's greatest triumph occurred in the 1950s with the ghoulish *Sunset Boulevard*. For the movie Swanson did her famous Charlie Chaplin imitation; murdered William Holden, who played her young screenwriter lover; and delivered the line, "We didn't need dialogue, we had faces." A self-prescribed health food freak, Gloria Swanson surfaced again in *Airport 1975.*

OPPOSITE: Swanson primps in full movie queen regalia—a velvet gown with fan train, crystal-beaded hip bands, and sequin panels; jet and crystal drop earrings; and a scarab headband entwined with her hair to form a turban.

BELOW: Because Swanson, at fifty, looked too good for her age in *Sunset Boulevard*, William Holden, thirty-one, had his make-up changed to make him look younger. When he remarks that she used to be a big star, the once and future movie queen pronounces, "I'm still big. It's the pictures that got small."

ABOVE: "The public, not I, made Gloria Swanson a star," declared Cecil B. DeMille, who directed her in *Why Change Your Wife?*—a kitschy clothes drama about a husband who looks elsewhere when his wife no longer dresses to please him.

LEFT: The Marquis de la Falaise de la Coudraye was Swanson's interpreter for *Madame Sans-Gêne*, made on location in France. "He was a gallant French nobleman, the kind every American woman dreams about," she remembered in her autobiography.

OPPOSITE: Raoul Walsh doubled as director and actor in the scorching *Sadie Thompson*, with Swanson as a prostitute in the South Seas. Her acting style was as exaggerated as her unusual combination of camera-proof features—an unmistakable pointed nose, projecting jaw line, and very large, wide eyes.

OPPOSITE: Swanson made an outrageous comeback in *Sunset Boulevard*. Playing himself, director Cecil B. DeMille welcomes the movie queen to his studio but gets out of making the film she has written. Swanson rattles off hilarious lines like, "The point is, I've never looked better in all my life." The hat she's wearing is of her own design.

BELOW: Movie icons never die, they get recycled as pop cinemabilia: the *Sunset Boulevard* drink coaster.

RIGHT: In remarkable condition for her age, the movie queen gestures with a single carnation in front of her portrait. An advocate of "you are what you eat and wear," Swanson had an operation to fix her eyes but never a face lift.

Rudolph Valentino
Latin Lover

Real name: Rodolpho Alfonso Raffaelo Pierre Filibert Guglielmi di Valentina d'Antonguolla
Born: May 6, 1895; Died: August 23, 1926

After seeing his films, wives and girl-friends complained to husbands and boyfriends about their awkward love-making. Though only movie make-believe, Rudolph Valentino's menacingly virile presence and animal sexuality threatened American men because it implied that they were lousy lovers. His escapist romances not only reflected the social changes brought about by World War I, but also signaled that women were ready for love, passion, and what *Fear of Flying* author, Erica Jong, called "the zipless fuck." The irony, of course, was that the fantasy lover couldn't deliver off-screen. The love he sought in his two

unconsummated marriages was merely a reflection of his love for himself.

What really set the tireless lady-killer's imagination racing was a costume. Donning the garb and gear of a gaucho, soldier, sheik, or bullfighter, Valentino became the man whose clothes he wore. A mixture of passion and melancholy, his gaze sent chills up and down female spines as his penetrating eyes promised exotic love.

The darkly handsome former gardener, dancer, and gigolo was catapulted into overnight stardom simply because his Latin Lover sex appeal was unprecedented. Before him, Latin men were cast as greasy villains. After

him, they symbolized fiery lovers whose prowess could satisfy women on and off the screen. A style-setter to the end, Valentino's early death at thirty-one transformed him into an instant legend.

OPPOSITE: As the desert chieftain in *The Son of the Sheik*, Valentino sweeps Vilma Banky off her feet. When the great lover came in for the clinch, his wild eyes protruded, his nostrils flared, and his sensuous lips parted temptingly as "the beloved," protesting virtuously but not too vehemently, succumbed.

BELOW: In *A Sainted Devil*, the idol's bedroom eyes telegraphed seduction.

Valentino commissioned Abbe, a famous photographer of the period, to do a series of portraits of him. This one exudes the star's grace, charisma, self-absorption, and love of beauty.

TOP: The Latin Lover takes good girl Lila Lee into his arms in *Blood and Sand*, about a famous bullfighter ruined by lust.

BOTTOM: The movie sex god dances the tango with Helena Domingues in *The Four Horsemen of the Apocalypse*.

RIGHT: Valentino and his second wife, set designer Natacha Rambova (born Winnifred Shaunessy), with Spanish painter Federico Beltram-Masses.

BELOW: When he died of peritonitis, Valentino, who squandered money extravagantly on clothes, horses, and baronial estates, was deeply in debt. Thousands grieved over his emaciated corpse, and he became the first superstar with a death cult.

Greta Garbo
The Face

Real name: Greta Louisa Gustafsson; Born: September 18, 1905
Academy Award: Special Oscar "for her unforgettable screen performances"

She stands alone as the immortal movie beauty. Like a moon goddess, the unmatchable Greta Garbo needed only to be seen to be worshipped. A new female type in films, she was regarded as "a cold-looking Nordic who exuded hot Latin passion." Women envied her ravishing beauty and the face any man could fall in love with. However, the much-imitated, strained languor that Garbo projected resulted in part from strenuous dieting enforced by studio bosses. Devotees never tired of trying to decipher the double riddle of how to uncover and fulfill whatever it was Garbo yearned for so desperately but could only hint at through her intoxicating gaze. Her elusive, enigmatic quality and unattainability were reinforced by the all-for-love stories of her formula "weepies." Audiences enjoyed watching the doomed *femme fatale* expire because they looked forward to her resurrection in the next heartbreaker.

If occasionally Greta Garbo's superficiality and selfishness peeked out from behind the mask, these traits only added to the fascination with her photographically exquisite face, which was flawless in shape and proportion. Black-and-white film intensified the alabaster whiteness of her skin. As cameraman William Daniels explained, "She was always taken in close-ups or long shots, hardly ever intermediate or full figure. The latter did not come out well."

Whether Garbo, the daughter of a poor Swedish laborer, consciously manipulated her air of mystery remains unknown. One theory contends that "the face" began to withdraw from the world when she started to speak in films—as if the last element of her personality was being taken from her. Unquestionably, her greatest mystique was that no man ever possessed her completely, making her all the more precious and eternally desirable. Garbo, who distrusted men, did not find an appropriate consort in either *Flesh and the Devil* co-star John Gilbert, whom she almost married, or photographer Cecil Beaton, who proposed.

The star retired from movies because she was disgusted with her anguished *femme fatale* roles. Having outlived peers, friends, and relatives, she remains "chained to an abnormal power of self-possession," which, some have suggested, is the biggest Greta Garbo mystery of all.

BELOW: After *Two-Faced Woman*, "the Swedish sphinx," who started her career as a Stockholm department store model, retired from films.

OPPOSITE: In *Wild Orchids*, Garbo's haunting eyes transfixed audiences.

LEFT: As the exotic spy in *Mata Hari*, Garbo follows her lover, Ramon Novarro, to death in front of a firing squad.

BELOW: In *Grand Hotel*, a coy Greta Garbo makes John Barrymore, a gentleman thief, fall in love with her and forget about stealing her jewels. When they first meet, she rebukes him with the line, "I want to be alone."

OPPOSITE: For *Camille*, her most beautiful and lavish "withering *femme fatale*" movie, Garbo was teamed with the equally beautiful Robert Taylor.

OPPOSITE: Garbo talked for the first time in *Anna Christie* and demanded, "Gimme a whiskey—ginger ale on the side—and don't be stingy, baby."

RIGHT: In sunglasses and fur coat, the divine recluse walks alone through the streets of Manhattan, where Garbo-watchers gawk but never dare to approach.

FAR RIGHT: A German factory worker turns out replicas of the film goddess's mask-like face. Other Garbo collectibles of the 1930s were postcards reproduced from movie stills and publicity photographs.

Peter the Tramp, 1922
The Saga of Gösta Berling, 1924
The Joyless Street, 1925
The Torrent, 1926
The Temptress, 1926
Flesh and the Devil, 1927
Love, 1927
The Divine Woman, 1928
The Mysterious Lady, 1928
A Woman of Affairs, 1929
Wild Orchids, 1929
The Single Standard, 1929
The Kiss, 1929
A Man's Man, 1929
Anna Christie, 1930
Romance, 1930
Inspiration, 1931
Susan Lenox: Her Fall and Rise, 1931
Mata Hari, 1931
Grand Hotel, 1932
As You Desire Me, 1932
Queen Christina, 1933
The Painted Veil, 1934
Anna Karenina, 1935
Camille, 1937
Conquest, 1937
Ninotchka, 1939
Two-Faced Woman, 1941

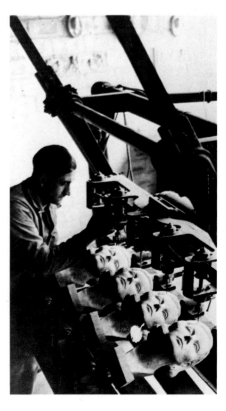

Errol Flynn
Swordsman

Real name: Errol Leslie Thomson Flynn; Born: June 20, 1909; Died: October 14, 1959

Celebrated for his amorous exploits and cardboard screen heroics, Errol Flynn excelled at playing the courageous daredevil swashbucklers Captain Blood, Robin Hood, and Don Juan, as well as the burned-out, degenerate alcoholics of *Too Much, Too Soon* and *The Sun Also Rises*. According to movie mogul Jack Warner, "To the Walter Mittys of the world, he was all the heroes in one magnificent sexy animal package."

The hellraiser's off-camera escapades hardly concealed a tortured and tormented Casanova. Flynn's impossible handsomeness and lack of discipline prevented him from exercising any form of self-control. Things came too easily to him and he valued little. For the reckless swordsman, life and movie acting were a game "not to be won but to go on to the next round."

Though he tried it three times, marriage was an intolerable institution for the free-wheeling womanizer. "It is hard for me to stay interested in any one woman in the world, no matter how fine she is," he said. Confessing to a fear and distrust of women, Flynn regretted that he never achieved with them the closeness and companionship he knew with men. Rumors of the sex champ's alleged homo- and bisexuality remain questionable, especially as he claimed his favorite occupation to be "a prolonged bout in the bedroom with a woman."

The source of Flynn's restlessness has been oversimplified in descriptions of his antagonistic relationship with his mother and his worship and admiration of his father, a distinguished marine biologist. The hedonistic playboy's decline commenced in the 1940s after he was acquitted of charges of statutory rape of two teenage girls. The expression "in like Flynn" became synonymous with the actor's living-phallic-symbol image and with the type of movie star who got away with murder.

Because Errol Flynn was incapable of taking himself seriously, no one else did either. The fickle and failed hero's heart attack at age fifty came as a surprise only because he lasted that long after years of consuming a fifth of vodka a day.

BELOW: As limited a writer as he was an actor, Flynn penned the first candid movie-superstar autobiography, *My Wicked, Wicked Ways*. In tell-all style, he wallowed in his confused personality, seamy love affairs, and self-destructive indulgences, forcing one reviewer to surmise that his "brains were in his pants."

OPPOSITE: The bandit of Sherwood Forest and his shadow duel with an unseen Sir Guy of Gisbourne (Basil Rathbone). The agile Flynn was proud of doing his own stunts—fencing, wall-scaling, vine-swinging—in *The Adventures of Robin Hood.*

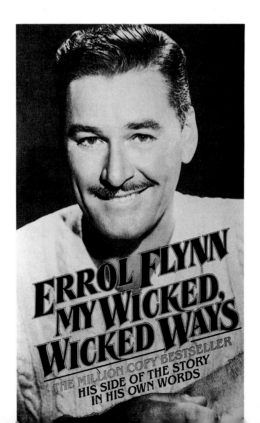

ABOVE: In *The Sea Hawk*, villain Henry Daniell temporarily outmaneuvers Errol Flynn.

LEFT: Along with dueling and being knighted, the swashbuckler's other forte was chivalrously rescuing Olivia De Havilland, his co-star in *Captain Blood* and six other movies. Flynn idealized her as a kind of perfect woman. "He was a charming and magnetic man," she said, "but so tormented."

OPPOSITE PAGE

TOP: In *The Sun Also Rises*, with Ava Gardner, Tyrone Power, and Eddie Albert, Flynn garnered raves for his all too realistic portrayal of a disintegrating alcoholic.

RIGHT TOP: "Women won't let me stay single and I won't let myself stay married," said the polyerotic Flynn. Complained wife Number One, Lili Damita, "You never know when he is telling the truth. He lies for the fun of it."

RIGHT CENTER: Nora Eddington, wife Number Two, was eighteen when she met Flynn. They had two daughters and divorced over his problems with liquor and drugs. Regarding his careless bravery, she noted, "He wasn't afraid of anything, particularly if there was a challenge to it."

RIGHT BOTTOM: Wife Number Three, Patrice Wymore, observed, "I don't think he should have married. He liked to be by himself or with his old cronies to chew the fat."

Marlene Dietrich Temptress

Real name: Maria Magdalene Dietrich; Born: December 27, 1901

When a wrist injury curtailed her violin career, conservatively brought up Marlene Dietrich switched to studying acting and joined the chorus line of a musical revue. But it was in the English and German language versions of *The Blue Angel* that her movie identity as the insatiable cabaret singer-temptress emerged, and overnight she materialized into an international-class film star.

Flashing her incredibly photogenic legs, covered in black stockings held up by a garter belt, and groaning the decadent "Falling in Love Again," Dietrich was devastating as the ruthless "blue angel" Lola-Lola. Producer Joe Pasternak summed up her emancipated she-devil impact in the film: "She was glamour personified. When she bestrode a stool and opened her legs, showing frilly pants, it was an almost brutal invitation.... She had the es-sential ingredient of international stardom: millions of guys would want to make love to her."

Most of Dietrich's roles were variations on temptress Lola-Lola. Fans of her gorgeous legs point out they were often the best things in her movies. No one smoked a cigarette or conveyed the fleetingness of life and *l'amour* as sexily as she did. In photographs and performances, Marlene Dietrich gave the impression of being a woman about to go off on an exciting and dangerous journey where unusual things were guaranteed to transpire.

Though she remained married to filmmaker turned chicken farmer Rudolf Seiber until his death in 1975, Dietrich had countless affairs. She sought the company of brilliant men—Jean Cocteau; novelist Erich Maria Remarque, who wrote *All Quiet on the Western Front*; and Ernest Heming-way, who referred to her as "the Kraut" and a "brave, generous, and loyal woman." For her valiant World War II front-line shows and anti-Nazi propaganda broadcasts, she received the U.S. Medal of Freedom and the French Legion of Honor.

As her film career waned in the 1950s, "the voice of the Lorelei" repackaged herself as a recording star and performer, singing international favorites in her acrid and husky dance-hall monotone. In her old age, Dietrich resides elegantly in Paris.

BELOW: In *The Blue Angel*, brassy night-club singer Lola-Lola humiliates and ruins Emil Jannings, an aging professor.

OPPOSITE: Dietrich's "What Becomes a Legend Most" look in *No Highway in the Sky*, in which she played Monica Teasdale, a cynical, glamorous film star.

ABOVE LEFT: Dietrich's white tie, tails, and top hat in *Morocco* became the sexually ambiguous side of her cabaret act. She showed her other side—and her beautiful figure—in a transparent gown.

ABOVE RIGHT: Playing yet another cabaret seductress in *Blonde Venus*, Dietrich, a devoted wife and mother, is forced to return to singing to earn money for her husband's medical treatments.

LEFT: Before falling in love with French Foreign Legionnaire Gary Cooper and following him into the desert, Dietrich, as singer Amy Jolly in *Morocco*, showed off her shapely legs, sang "What Am I Bid for My Apples," and placed a shocking kiss on the mouth of a woman in the nightclub audience.

LEFT: Interrogated by Charles Laughton in *Witness for the Prosecution*, Dietrich gave a *tour de force* performance. Her testimony saves her unworthy husband, Tyrone Power, charged with the murder of a rich widow.

BELOW: Dietrich the *chanteuse* packed houses in Las Vegas, Moscow, London, and Paris with her throaty renditions of "Lili Marlene," "You're the Cream in My Coffee," "See What the Boys in the Back Room Will Have," and "I Wish You Love." These appearances were notable for her sixty-second change from elaborate gown to tuxedo.

For Dietrich's 1923–29 films, see page 271

The Blue Angel, 1930
Morocco, 1930
Dishonored, 1931
Shanghai Express, 1932
Blonde Venus, 1932
Song of Songs, 1933
The Scarlet Empress, 1934
The Devil Is a Woman, 1935
Desire, 1936
The Garden of Allah, 1936
Knight Without Armor, 1937
Angel, 1937
Destry Rides Again, 1939
Seven Sinners, 1940
The Flame of New Orleans, 1941
Manpower, 1941
The Lady Is Willing, 1942
The Spoilers, 1942
Pittsburgh, 1942
Follow the Boys, 1944
Kismet, 1944
The Room Upstairs, 1946
Golden Earrings, 1947
A Foreign Affair, 1948
Jigsaw, 1949
Stage Fright, 1950
No Highway in the Sky, 1951
Rancho Notorious, 1952
Around the World in 80 Days, 1956
The Monte Carlo Story, 1957
Witness for the Prosecution, 1957
Touch of Evil, 1958
Judgment at Nuremberg, 1961
Black Fox, 1962
Paris When It Sizzles, 1964
Just a Gigolo, 1978

Clark Gable
The King

Real name: William Clark Gable; Born: February 1, 1901; Died: November 16, 1960
Academy Award: Best Actor, It Happened One Night

He wore the crown and title of "he-man king" lightly and stuck to his promise that success would not change the size of his hat. Gable was the first superstar to play himself. With his tom-cat grin, raven black hair, and gray-green eyes, the "giant economy-size prince" took America by storm. He treated women roughly in movies and made it clear that he would accept them on his terms or not at all, a condition that spilled over into his private life. When the king smacked or spanked a leading lady it meant, "I want you and you're mine."

The likable Gable wanted the same things from life that the average Depression-era Joe did—a job, a wife, and security. Grateful for work in the movies (he was turned down at first because his ears were too big), the workhorse was thankful to be typecast and didn't moan about wishing he were back on Broadway, where he'd known some success. When the one-time oil-rigger, lumberjack, and farmer became an independent star in the fifties, he was asked if he planned to direct films. "Hell, no," the king replied, "I haven't even learned how to act yet."

Gable was supposedly reluctant to accept the part of Rhett Butler in *Gone With the Wind*, the film that served as his coronation ceremony. Though he didn't mind insulting Scarlett O'Hara with "Frankly, my dear, I don't give a damn," he had to be convinced that crying over her miscarriage would not be out of character. If anything, the gesture magnified his manliness, confirming he could be husband, father, lover, brother, and friend to a woman.

Gable married two types of women: older mother-teachers and sweetheart-companions. (In between, the king engaged in a thousand one-night stands with car hops and manicurists.) Women agreed that his greatest asset was making them feel he appreciated them as both a female and a person. But he insisted that his wife be a well-dressed, gracious hostess and be ready for sex with him whenever he was in the mood. He never got over the death of his third wife, dizzy screwball comedy princess Carole Lombard, who shared his love of practical jokes. Her best replacement, look-alike Kay Spreckles, had Gable's only son, John Clark Gable, shortly after the king's death from a heart condition.

OPPOSITE: In *Gone With the Wind*, Rhett Butler (Clark Gable) plants one on bitchy Scarlett O'Hara (Vivien Leigh).

BELOW: Over the last four decades, the king's he-man image has worn well during re-releases of the Civil War super-epic.

ABOVE: Claudette Colbert and Clark Gable share a room in *It Happened One Night*.

LEFT: The big-eared lunk with kinky Jean Harlow in *Hold Your Man*.

OPPOSITE PAGE

LEFT: The King and Carole Lombard at a movie premiere. When they met, Gable's opening line was, "I go for you, Maw." Lombard volleyed back, "I go for you, Paw."

RIGHT: Co-stars Montgomery Clift, Marilyn Monroe, and Gable on the set of *The Misfits*. Behind them: Eli Wallach, Arthur Miller, and director John Huston.

OVERLEAF: Rhett Butler dances with Scarlett O'Hara in *Gone With The Wind*.

White Man, 1924
Forbidden Paradise, 1924
The Pacemakers, 1925
The Merry Widow, 1925
The Plastic Age, 1925
North Star, 1926
The Painted Desert, 1931
The Easiest Way, 1931
Dance, Fools, Dance, 1931
The Secret Six, 1931
The Finger Points, 1931
Laughing Sinners, 1931
A Free Soul, 1931
Night Nurse, 1931
Sporting Blood, 1931
Susan Lenox: Her Fall and Rise, 1931
Possessed, 1931
Hell Divers, 1931
Polly of the Circus, 1932
Strange Interlude, 1932
Red Dust, 1932
No Man of Her Own, 1932
The White Sister, 1933
Hold Your Man, 1933
Night Flight, 1933

Dancing Lady, 1933
It Happened One Night, 1934
Men in White, 1934
Manhattan Melodrama, 1934
Chained, 1934
Forsaking All Others, 1934
After Office Hours, 1935
Call of the Wild, 1935
China Seas, 1935
Mutiny on the Bounty, 1935
Wife vs. Secretary, 1936
San Francisco, 1936
Cain and Mabel, 1936
Love on the Run, 1936
Parnell, 1937
Saratoga, 1937
Test Pilot, 1938
Too Hot to Handle, 1938
Idiot's Delight, 1939
Gone With the Wind, 1939
Strange Cargo, 1940
Boom Town, 1940
Comrade X, 1940
They Met in Bombay, 1941
Honky Tonk, 1941

Somewhere I'll Find You, 1942
Adventure, 1945
The Hucksters, 1947
Homecoming, 1948
Command Decision, 1948
Any Number Can Play, 1949
Key to the City, 1950
To Please a Lady, 1950
Across the Wide Missouri, 1951
Callaway Went Thataway,
  1951
Lone Star, 1952
Never Let Me Go, 1953
Mogambo, 1953
Betrayed, 1954
Soldier of Fortune, 1955
The Tall Men, 1955
The King and Four Queens,
  1956
Band of Angels, 1957
Run Silent, Run Deep, 1958
Teacher's Pet, 1958
But Not for Me, 1959
It Started in Naples, 1960
The Misfits, 1961

53

Mae West
Bombshell

Real name: Mary Jane West; Born: August 17, 1893; Died: November 25, 1980

Sex Queen. Camp Vamp. Female Satyr. Sexual Pioneer. First Female Chauvinist Pig. Geriatric Sex Symbol. "There had never been anybody like me before," insisted the flamboyant and irreverent Mae "Any time you got nothing to do—and lots of time to do it—come on up" West. The earthy comedienne let all kinds of sex out of the closet with her self-kidding witticisms and raunchy double entendres. Her philosophy, "An orgasm a day keeps the doctor away," was promulgated in her movies by toned-down one-liners—"It's not the men in my life but the life in my men," and "Too much of a good thing can be wonderful."

West's style relied on the principle that it's what you don't reveal and the way you say what you say that keeps men interested. Her golden rule was Mae West first, last, and always. She made no bones about the fact that she communicated with men by sleeping with them. Her stable of on- and off-camera studs was composed of boxers, wrestlers, and weight lifters of all races.

A phenomenon in every way, West quit school in third grade, performed as a baby vamp in talent contests, had her first sexual experience before puberty, and wrote a play about homosexuality called *The Drag*. Everything the bombshell did was light years ahead of her times: she reversed sex roles (she's the leading man and Cary Grant the delectable beauty in *She Done Him Wrong*); she stuffed her night club act with body builders before male stripteasers were thought of; and she made sure her message about the double standard applying to both sexes got across. A larger-than-life sexual institution, Mae West has been overexplained as a pre-Freudian woman, a forerunner of the Me Decade, and a mechanical sexual athlete with a double thyroid. One in a zillion, her success was a fluke.

For the last twenty-seven years of her life, West settled into an older woman-younger man relationship with Paul Novak, a gentle and devoted muscle man. "I believe I was put on this earth to take care of Miss West," remarked her combination bodyguard, lover, chauffeur, secretary, and companion.

A great aphorist, Mae West was also an astute observer of male and female psychology. "Women," she said, "are as old as they feel—and men are old when they lose their feelings."

BELOW: For her final film, *Sextette*, a grotesque bedroom farce, West, who was in her eighties, recruited Tony Curtis, Ringo Starr, George Hamilton, and an army of muscle men, including this one.

OPPOSITE: The buxom comedienne brought the hip-swinging Jezebel of her play *Diamond Lil* to the screen in *She Done Him Wrong*, redefining attitudes toward female sexuality with the line, "When women go wrong, men go right after 'em."

OPPOSITE: La West at seventy-five reclines on a chaise in her Hollywood apartment. It's rumored the sex queen derived great pleasure from watching herself in the mirrored ceiling and wall of her landmark gold and white bed. Her autoeroticism has been cited as proof of hidden insecurity. Cary Grant noted, "She wanted to be responsible for everything. She dealt in a fantasy world. The heavy makeup she wore was a sign of her insecurity. We were all very careful with her."

TOP: "I understand you need a cicerone—a guide," W.C. Fields suggests to Mae West in *My Little Chickadee*. "I need more than that, honey," she cuts in.

CENTER: As Tira, a honky-tonk singer-dancer and lion tamer in *I'm No Angel*, West put her head into a tranquilized lion's mouth (her secret ambition had always been to be a lion tamer). Also noteworthy were the movie's Westicisms: "Beulah, peel me a grape," and "When I'm good, I'm very good, but when I'm bad, I'm better."

BOTTOM: "If he can talk, I'll take him," claimed Mae, who was so captured by Cary Grant's good looks that she cast him as the Salvation Army reformer in *She Done Him Wrong*. Their chemistry and the West-supplied dialogue were delicious. Cary: "Haven't you ever met a man who could make you happy?" Mae: "Sure. Lots of times."

Night After Night, 1932
She Done Him Wrong, 1933
I'm No Angel, 1933
Belle of the Nineties, 1934
Goin' to Town, 1935
Klondike Annie, 1936
Go West Young Man, 1936
Every Day's a Holiday, 1938
My Little Chickadee, 1940
The Heat's On, 1943
Myra Breckenridge, 1970
Sextette, 1978

W. C. Fields Cynic

Real name: William Claude Dukenfield; Born: January 29, 1880; Died: December 25, 1946

With his bulging belly, swollen red schnoz, and piggy eyes that judged everything, the rowdy and obstreperous W.C. Fields was a riot as a con artist or a henpecked husband. The first completely American character to appear in talking pictures, the old lecher's avocations were loafing, drinking, and holding forth at the "Black Pussy Cat Café." Cigar in one hand and drink in the other, he carried mouthing off from a national pastime to an art form. By turning normal family relations upside down, his black humor debunked the hypocrisy of middle-class American attitudes. So famous did his declamatory phrases become that "Any man who hates children and dogs can't be all that bad" was attributed to Fields even though it was said about him by a friend.

In a scornful whiskey drawl, he slipped irascible one-liners, funny euphemisms, and ridiculous nomenclatures out of the side of his mouth. His enduring popularity—people still laugh at the mention of his name—derived from unexpected appellations and convoluted tongue-twisters like "My ravishing little pineapple," "My little Mexican jumping bean," and "I shall dally in the valley, and believe me I can dally" from *International House*. In the ticklish western parody *My Little Chickadee*, the great misogynist met the great man eater. A match made in movie heaven was consummated with W.C. Fields's horny banter and asides and Mae West's racy double entendres and dialogue.

Regretting that he had ever been born, Fields left home permanently at age eleven and eventually became a successful comedy juggler in vaudeville and a Broadway star. Past fifty when he made his best-remembered "talkies," he grew wealthy but always worried about money and suffered from insomnia. Antisocial and a heavy drinker ("I never drink anything stronger than gin before breakfast."), the king of comedy fluctuated between seclusion and partying.

Lines from his ludicrous movies readily come to mind, and it's easy to mimic Fields because he's the cranky sardonic individualist in all of us. At the time of his death, the author of *Fields for President* was working on a screenplay entitled *Grand Motel*.

BELOW: In *My Little Chickadee*, Mae West (Flower Belle Lee) marries W.C. Fields (Cuthbert J. Twillie) and substitutes a goat for herself in their wedding bed.

OPPOSITE: Fields tried to work his juggling routine into the role of Wilkins Micawber in the movie of Charles Dickens's *David Copperfield*. Told by producer David O. Selznick that Dickens had not written anything about Micawber juggling, Fields grunted, "He probably forgot it."

LEFT: In *The Fatal Glass of Beer*, Fields beats his son Chester and kicks him out into the snow, shouting, "It ain't a fit night out for man or beast!"

BELOW: Queried as to whether he liked children, Fields once responded, "Only if they are properly cooked." But in films like *Never Give a Sucker an Even Break*, the Swiftian humorist was more often the victim than the tormentor of brats like Butch and Buddy.

ABOVE: Under a variety of wacky noms de plume, Fields concocted wildly improbable plots like the one for *The Bank Dick* (by Mahatma Kane Jeeves) in which the put-upon family man takes over for a drunken director and then becomes a hero when a bank robber trips over him.

RIGHT: Notorious for his love of alcohol, the comic insisted, "It was a woman that drove me to drink and I never had the decency to thank her."

FAR RIGHT: Carlotta Monti was W.C. Fields's companion and mistress during the last fourteen years of his life. She wrote *W.C. Fields and Me*, a book that was turned into a dreadful "bio-pic."

ABOVE: Cheating at cards—a Fields specialty. "Is this a game of chance?" someone asked in *My Little Chickadee*. "Not the way I play it," he snorted.

BELOW: A fitting tribute—the cocktail napkin from a bar in Philadelphia, the city of Fields's birth and the source of his most remembered pet peeve. As his con-

tribution to *Vanity Fair* magazine's "write your own epitaph" roundup, the comedian penned the much misquoted expression, "I would rather be living in Philadelphia."

Pool Sharks, 1915
His Lordship's Dilemma, 1915
Janice Meredith, 1924
Sally of the Sawdust, 1925
That Royle Girl, 1926
It's the Old Army Game, 1926
So's Your Old Man, 1926
The Potters, 1927
Running Wild, 1927
Two Flaming Youths, 1927
Tillie's Punctured Romance, 1928
Fools for Luck, 1928
The Golf Specialist, 1930
Her Majesty Love, 1931
Million Dollar Legs, 1932
If I Had a Million, 1932
The Dentist, 1932
The Fatal Glass of Beer, 1933
The Pharmacist, 1933
The Barber Shop, 1933
Hip Action, 1933
International House, 1933

Tillie and Gus, 1933
Alice in Wonderland, 1933
Six of a Kind, 1934
You're Telling Me, 1934
The Old-Fashioned Way, 1934
Mrs. Wiggs of the Cabbage Patch, 1934
It's a Gift, 1934
David Copperfield, 1935
Mississippi, 1935
The Man on the Flying Trapeze, 1935
Poppy, 1936
The Big Broadcast of 1938, 1938
You Can't Cheat an Honest Man, 1939
My Little Chickadee, 1940
The Bank Dick, 1940
Never Give a Sucker an Even Break, 1941
Tales of Manhattan, 1942
Follow the Boys, 1944
Song of the Open Road, 1944
Sensations of 1945, 1944

In the Continental Building on Fourth at Market

The Incomparables

Ginger Rogers and Fred Astaire
King and Queen of Dance

"He gives her class and she gives him sex."
— A 1930s aphorism about Fred Astaire and Ginger Rogers attributed to Katharine Hepburn.

When wisecracking chorus girl Ginger Rogers and debonair hoofer Fred Astaire tilted to and fro to the snappy rhythms of "The Carioca," movie dancing became art.

LEFT: In *Gold Diggers of 1933* (minus Astaire), spunky Ginger Rogers sang one verse of "We're in the Money" in pig Latin.

RIGHT: In *Top Hat*, the essential Fred Astaire in white tie, black tails with boutonniere, cane, and tap Oxfords.

OPPOSITE: "We'll show 'em a thing or three," boasted Ginger Rogers as she and Fred fast-tangoed to "The Carioca" in their first musical, *Flying Down to Rio.* The object of the trick dance was for the partners to execute a complete turn without breaking head contact.

The most elegant "ideal love team" in film history, Fred Astaire and Ginger Rogers showed that the way to a swell romance began with a dance. One glimpse of the flighty Ginger, and the nonchalant Fred goes into a tailspin. Only by dancing with her can Astaire possess Rogers, and she succumbs to the only partner in the world who can dance her to "heaven." The Astaire–Rogers love scenes are their pulsating dances—the sleek ballroom duets, the rapturous balletic adagios, the glorious tap duels, the athletic challenge dances, and the breezy novelty numbers. Decked out in high-class, *haute couture* finery, the king and queen of dance glided through a Never-Never Land of ballrooms that expanded into what seemed like outer space. Rogers's finesse eventually matched Astaire's in the competition dances "I'll Be Hard to Handle" and "Pick Yourself Up." His incredible solos,"Bojangles of Harlem" and "Slap That Bass," set the criteria future movie dancers would aspire to. But it is the harmony of their love dances — "Night and Day," "Cheek to Cheek," and "Change Partners"— that all of us secretly imitate when we dance to reruns of the Astaire–Rogers musicals in front of our television sets.

OPPOSITE: The king and queen of dance atop seven pianos for "The Carioca" production number in *Flying Down to Rio*.

BELOW: Shot in one take, *Swing Time*'s celebratory "Waltz in Swing Time" is bliss.

RIGHT: Swaying to "The Continental" in *The Gay Divorcee*, Ginger and Fred follow the song's lovely instruction to "kiss while you're dancing."

THE ECSTASY: The raffish "Let's Face the Music and Dance," *Follow the Fleet*

THE RAPTURE: The exhausting Castle Walk "Too Much Mustard," *The Story of Vernon and Irene Castle*

ABOVE: In *The Barkleys of Broadway*, the king and queen of dance parted forever with the splashy "Manhattan Downbeat" finale.

LEFT: Danced during the credits of *The Barkleys of Broadway*, "The Swing Trot," a Fred and Ginger cocktail of ballroom and show biz choreography, is still used in advertisements for the Fred Astaire Dance Studios.

RIGHT: Marking the donation of the RKO Studios' Archives to U.C.L.A., Rogers and Astaire do a turn in front of a poster of one of their classic dance musicals.

Using the ballet principles of balance and grace as jumping-off points, Fred Astaire's breathless choreography revolutionized movie dancing. Before him, dancers were photographed in pieces —their heads and feet patched together in the cutting room. Astaire insisted on being filmed full figure. A natural-born dance drill sergeant and movie engineer, he upgraded camera work, cutting, and the synchronization and scoring of his movie dances, which averaged three minutes, to standards of his own precision.

Mr. A and Miss R, as they were called on the set, never let feuds over her feathered gowns and high heels get in the way of their sublime collaborations. "The Continental" and "The Piccolino"—galvanizing production numbers on the big white sets that Depression-era audiences sighed over—gave way to the thrilling romantic duets. In *The Barkleys of Broadway*, Fred, fifty, and Ginger, thirty-eight, ended their partnership in prime condition.

ABOVE: In the dance comedy *Carefree*, Astaire flips Rogers into a spiraling lift as they execute "The Yam" strut.

RIGHT: In tweeds and roller skates, Astaire and Rogers skate and tap dance to "Let's Call the Whole Thing Off" in *Shall We Dance*. During the fantastic number, the quarreling couple (she says "eether," he says eyether") clack out their disagreement in an amazing duel on wheels.

Flying Down to Rio, 1933
The Gay Divorcee, 1934
Roberta, 1935
Top Hat, 1935
Follow the Fleet, 1936
Swing Time, 1936
Shall We Dance, 1937
Carefree, 1938
The Story of Vernon and Irene Castle, 1939
The Barkleys of Broadway, 1949

For Rogers's films, see page 77
For Astaire's films, see page 83

Ginger Rogers
Chorus Girl

Real name: Virginia Katherine McMath; Born: July 16, 1911
Academy Award: Best Actress, Kitty Foyle

The Charleston champ from Texas came on with a bang in *Young Man of Manhattan* when she cracked the line, "Cigarette me, Big Boy!" But it was as chorus girls Fay Fortune in *Gold Diggers of 1933* and Anytime Annie Lowell in *42nd Street* that Ginger Rogers became the "American pie" glamour girl of the 1930s. After the royal Astaire–Rogers musicals, she clicked in *Bachelor Mother* and *Kitty Foyle*, soap opera fables about white-collar working girls. Her best performances combined "her screwball comedy acting and fairytale play acting," which reflected her own positive-thinking disposition (she had a soda fountain installed in her Beverly Hills mansion).

After her working-class princesses went out of style, Rogers became a fashion consultant to the J.C. Penney department-store chain and took over the leads in the Broadway musicals *Mame* and *Hello, Dolly!* Faithful fans flocked to her nostalgic 1970s night club revue that concluded with a tribute to Fred Astaire. From time to time, the queen of chorus girls drops in for special shows with the Rockettes at her true home—Radio City Music Hall.

BELOW: In the lightweight *Lady in the Dark*, Ginger Rogers is a magazine editor who undergoes psychoanalysis to find out why she suffers from headaches and daydreams.

OPPOSITE: As a working girl from a lower-middle-class family in *Kitty Foyle*, Rogers was romanced by Dennis Morgan, who played a Philadelphia socialite.

For Rogers's films with Fred Astaire, see page 73

Ginger Rogers rehearsing with chorus boys in top hats, canes, and "Will you be my Fred?" sweatshirts for her night club act, which included a young Ginger Rogers impersonator and a comic. Kissing a top hat, she closed the show with "Good night, Fred."

Fred Astaire
Hoofer

Real name: Frederick Austerlitz; Born: May 10, 1899
Academy Award: Special Oscar for "his unique artistry and his contributions
to the technique of motion pictures"

For over fifty years, Fred Astaire's punctuated choreography interpreted every dance from the fox trot to jitterbug and rock and roll. When his sister Adele, his best-matched partner, married Lord Charles Cavendish and ended their successful comedy-dance stage act, Astaire hightailed it to Hollywood despite the screen-test report card: "Can't act. Slightly bald. Can dance a little." The hoofer preferred movie to stage musicals because he could control the mechanics of his dance magic. He topped the Astaire-Rogers glory days with a long career of spectacular dance solos and films

with Gene Kelly, Rita Hayworth, Judy Garland, Leslie Caron, and Cyd Charisse, whom he dubbed "beautiful dynamite" because of her marvelous precision.

Secretly, the dance king wanted to be a musician, probably a drummer, and a combination dance-band-leader/vocalist. Aficionados consider his fey, funny-sounding voice the height of sophistication. But it is Astaire's quicksilver gift for keeping perfect time to music that's remarkable in his self-styled jazz, ballet, and tap combinations and his fanciful, one-of-a-kind choreography like *Royal Wedding*'s

gravity-defying "You're All the World to Me." The last lines of Fred Astaire's biography, *Steps in Time*, explain him best. "I have no desire to prove anything by it. . . . I just dance."

BELOW: The sparkling Astaires—Adele, seventeen, and Fred, sixteen—dazzled London and Broadway audiences with their charm and comedy-dance routines.

OPPOSITE: The "Shoes with Wings On" solo from The *Barkleys of Broadway*.

OVERLEAF: *Blue Skies*' "Puttin' on the Ritz" finds the hoofer dancing with a line of special effects Astaires.

OPPOSITE: One of Astaire's great four-in-the-morning ideas, "You're All the World to Me" from *Royal Wedding*. The workout involved tricky mechnical photography and revolving scenery for his upside-down-on-the-ceiling-and-around-the-walls choreography.

ABOVE: Astaire admired Judy Garland's intuitive showmanship. In *Easter Parade*, they sang and strolled along Fifth Avenue.

Cyd Charisse and Fred Astaire set off sparks in *The Band Wagon* with the dramatic and splashy "Girl Hunt Ballet." The number, inspired by the Mickey Spillane detective story thrillers, is regarded as one of the most imaginative examples of Astaire's numerous dance styles.

BELOW: The hoofer, a race horse enthusiast, and his second wife, jockey Robyn Smith.

Dancing Lady, 1933
A Damsel in Distress, 1937
Broadway Melody of 1940, 1940
Second Chorus, 1940
You'll Never Get Rich, 1941
Holiday Inn, 1942
You Were Never Lovelier, 1942
The Sky's the Limit, 1943
Yolanda and the Thief, 1945
Ziegfeld Follies, 1946
Blue Skies, 1946
Easter Parade, 1948
Three Little Words, 1950
Let's Dance, 1950
Royal Wedding, 1951
The Belle of New York, 1952

The Band Wagon, 1953
Daddy Long Legs, 1955
Funny Face, 1957
Silk Stockings, 1957
On the Beach, 1959
The Pleasure of His Company, 1961
The Notorious Landlady, 1962
Finian's Rainbow, 1968
Midas Run, 1969
Imagine, 1973
That's Entertainment, 1974
The Towering Inferno, 1974
That's Entertainment, Part II, 1976
The Amazing Dobermans, 1976
Ghost Story, 1981
A Purple Taxi, 1982

For Astaire's films with Ginger Rogers, see page 73

The Marx Brothers
Mass Hysteria

HARPO
Adolph Marx
November 23, 1888–
September 28, 1964

ZEPPO
Herbert Marx
February 25, 1901–
November 29, 1979

CHICO
Leonard Marx
August 21, 1887–
October 11, 1961

GROUCHO
Julius Henry Marx
October 2, 1890–
August 19, 1977

Comedy of the ridiculous came to the movies with the nutsy Marx Brothers, who piled improvised and orchestrated slapstick on top of idiotic mischief and glued the insanity together with goofy insults and puns.

BELOW: In *Monkey Business*, stowaways Harpo, Zeppo, Chico, and Groucho harmonized "Sweet Adeline" and tried to get off a boat by pretending, in turn, to be Maurice Chevalier.

Salvador Dali, who wrote the script *The Marx Brothers on Horseback Salad*, championed their surrealistic anarchy and nonsensical humor. Appealing to highbrows and lowbrows alike, the pranksters ridiculed high society, the medical profession, and The Establishment.

With his famous slouch, Groucho took the lead, spouting non sequiturs, abuses ("We're fighting for this woman's honor, which is more than she ever did."), and terrible puns ("The lord Alps those who Alp themselves."). Harpo, the mute trickster, hit people with hammers and lighted cigars with a blowtorch. Happy-go-lucky Chico caused problems by refusing to take anything seriously. Zeppo, the inept straight man, appeared in five comedies, and Gummo, the fifth brother, never appeared in any of their films.

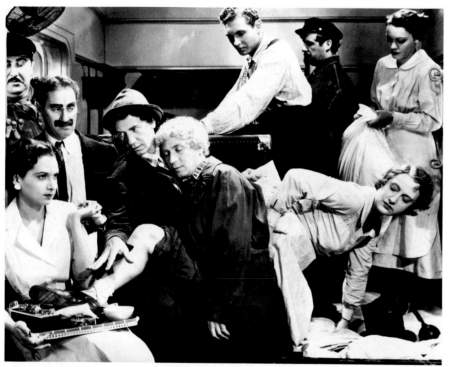

TOP: With Harpo and Chico as assistants, Groucho, as horse doctor Hugo Z. Hackenbush, examines hypochrondriac Margaret Dumont in *A Day at the Races*.

CENTER: In *A Night at the Opera*, the boys squeezed into a ship's tiny stateroom with the engineer's assistant, a girl looking for her Aunt Minnie, and seven other unrelated people.

BOTTOM: In *Go West*, Groucho attempts to sell Harpo the latest in Western fashion as Chico looks on.

OPPOSITE: In *The Cocoanuts*, Groucho at the feet of Margaret Dumont.

Too Many Kisses, 1925
The Cocoanuts, 1929
Animal Crackers, 1930
Monkey Business, 1931
Horse Feathers, 1932
Duck Soup, 1933
A Night at the Opera, 1935
A Day at the Races, 1937
Room Service, 1938
At the Circus, 1939
Go West, 1940
The Big Store, 1941
Stage Door Canteen, 1943
A Night in Casablanca, 1946
Love Happy, 1950
The Story of Mankind, 1957

For Groucho's films, see p. 88

Academy Award to Groucho Marx: Special Oscar "in recognition of his brilliant creativity and the unparalleled achievements of the Marx Brothers in the art of motion picture comedy"

Although their television pilot "Deputy Seraph" didn't get off the ground, the Marx Brothers' wacky antics continue to be a major influence on television comedy. After they broke up, Groucho became the most famous Marx Brother. From 1950 to 1961 he hosted the frenetic comedy quiz show "You Bet Your Life." The familiar Groucho mustache (his own—the one in the movies was painted on) and cigar were weapons for his attacks on contestants. Ruder and funnier than ever, Groucho teased certain players about their unusual occupations and backgrounds and egged them on to win an extra $101 for "saying the secret word"—a common household word like "asparagus."

RIGHT: The lecherous Groucho with Sarita Pelkey, the kind of well-endowed contestant he liked on "You Bet Your Life."

BELOW: "What! From Africa to here, a dollar eighty-five?" Groucho barks as the African explorer Captain Geoffrey T. Spaulding in *Animal Crackers.* Groucho fractured audiences with his entrance on a sedan chair and lines like "Africa is God's country, and He can have it." The song "Hooray for Captain Spaulding" became the theme music for his television show.

Copacabana, 1947
Mister Music, 1950
Double Dynamite, 1951
A Girl in Every Port, 1952
Will Success Spoil Rock Hunter?, 1957
Skidoo, 1968

The Originals

Joan Crawford
Working Girl

Real Name: Lucille Fay LeSueur (a.k.a. Billie Cassin)
Born: March 23, 1906; Died: May 10, 1977
Academy Award: Best Actress, Mildred Pierce

Life and movies were a trial by fire for ambitious Lucille LeSueur, who became Joan Crawford when the name was chosen for her in a movie magazine contest. Her emotionally unstable but adaptable and determined working girls and tough-talking career women were consumed by their quest for upward mobility. Crawford's school of-hard-knocks melodramas (*Possessed, Grand Hotel, Harriet Craig*) were training manuals on how to get a piece, if not all, of the American pie.

What her women with masculine drives resented was not being given access to opportunity—the birthright of men. Prepared to sacrifice all in their climb from poverty to Park Avenue luxury, these overachievers failed to recognize the flaw in the scenario. They were still the same people with the same unsolved problems after they got what they thought they were after.

Describing herself as a "strict disciplinarian" to her adopted son and three daughters, Joan Crawford acknowledged that Hollywood kids got the dirty end of the stick because stars wanted their careers more than they did happy home lives. She blamed the drinking during her endless menopause years on "money problems and career problems."

The star died on the anniversary of her marriage to her last husband, Alfred Steele, an executive of Pepsi-Cola, the company she served as a board member and publicity spokeswoman during her second career. Although the cause of Crawford's death was listed as cardiac arrest, friends attributed it to heartbreak.

LEFT: Crawford felt her role in *Mildred Pierce* was a composite of all her fallen women and suffering sinners. She does everything for her ungrateful, spoiled daughter, Ann Blyth, including confess to the girl's murder of her stepfather.

BELOW: Adopted daughter Christina Crawford's horrifying best seller *Mommie Dearest* portrayed her movie-star mother as a child abuser who was herself abused as a child.

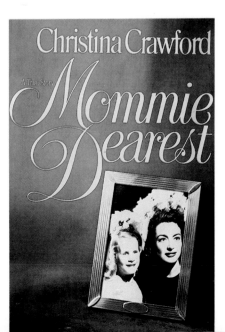

LEFT: A typical flaming youth-of-the-1920s flick, *Our Dancing Daughters* made jazz-baby Crawford a star.

BELOW LEFT: In *Possessed*, Joan Crawford played a small-town factory worker who becomes involved with Clark Gable, a rich and powerful attorney.

BELOW RIGHT: The tables turn on Crawford in *Sudden Fear*. She's a wealthy play-wright hustled by a younger man, who plans to kill her for her money.

OPPOSITE: Cleanaholic Crawford mops up while talking to a guest after a party in her New York apartment. Tales of the movie star's compulsive cleanliness are legion. She once lost a maid because she demanded that a tree outside her window be scrubbed and waxed.

Humphrey Bogart Tough Guy

Real name: Humphrey DeForest Bogart; Born: January 23, 1899; Died: January 14, 1957
Academy Award: Best Actor, The African Queen

Before the type became fashionable, Humphrey Bogart's tough-guy hero was "a cool cat with soul." He represented disillusionment and the notion that something had gone wrong with the world. As the hard-boiled detective with the snarling lisp, the Bogey character was above profiting from other people's corruption.

It was Bogey's way or no way. Audiences ate up the "don't mess with me" mystique of his heroes, who were true to their own moral and ethical code and didn't know the meaning of an identity crisis. The way he exhaled cigarette smoke and extinguished a butt was as lethal as his pistol whippings.

An opinionated man, Humphrey Bogart maintained that an actor owed an audience a good performance, and nothing more. He enjoyed drinking, mistrusted anyone who didn't drink, and believed the only reason to have money was to be able "to tell any s.o.b. in the world to go to hell." An abrasive needler, he tested strangers, friends, and wives to see how they measured up.

When he met Lauren Bacall, his future co-star and wife, the sour tough guy informed the undulating siren: "I saw your test. We'll have a lot of fun together." The sex talk of their films became widely emulated, especially Bacall's famous line to Bogey in *To Have and Have Not*: "You know how to whistle, don't you Steve. You just put your lips together and blow."

Bogart liked to tell friends that the happiest time of his life was "when I was courting Betty." Their nine-year marriage ended when the legendary Bogey died of cancer.

BELOW: As detective Sam Spade in *The Maltese Falcon*, Bogey derides the fake black statuette of the falcon as "the stuff dreams are made of."

OPPOSITE: Protecting Mary Astor in *Across the Pacific*, Humphrey Bogart whips out a revolver and adopts his tough guy stance.

ABOVE: Dooley Wilson plays "As Time Goes By" in *Casablanca* as Bogey pours a drink for Ingrid Bergman. The part of the weary café owner, Rick, made Bogart a romantic figure, representing every guy who had ever been hurt by a woman.

LEFT: Katharine Hepburn, a determined missionary, and Humphrey Bogart, a skeptical drunk, made an unlikely pair of adventurers in *The African Queen*. They destroy a German gunboat that's holding an invasion route against British forces in World War I.

Bogart and Lauren Bacall in *Dark Passage*.

The Bogarts with Steven and Leslie.

A Devil With Women, 1930
Up the River, 1930
Body and Soul, 1931
Bad Sister, 1931
Women of All Nations, 1931
A Holy Terror, 1931
Love Affair, 1932
Big City Blues, 1932
Three on a Match, 1932
Midnight, 1934
The Petrified Forest, 1936
Bullets or Ballots, 1936
Two Against the World, 1936
China Clipper, 1936
Isle of Fury, 1936
Black Legion, 1937
The Great O'Malley, 1937
Marked Woman, 1937
Kid Galahad, 1937
San Quentin, 1937
Dead End, 1937
Stand-In, 1937
Swing Your Lady, 1938
Crime School, 1938
Men Are Such Fools, 1938
The Amazing Dr. Clitterhouse, 1938

Racket Busters, 1938
Angels With Dirty Faces, 1938
King of the Underworld, 1939
The Oklahoma Kid, 1939
Dark Victory, 1939
You Can't Get Away With Murder, 1939
The Roaring Twenties, 1939
The Return of Dr. X, 1939
Invisible Stripes, 1939
Virginia City, 1940
It All Came True, 1940
Brother Orchid, 1940
They Drive by Night, 1940
High Sierra, 1941
The Wagons Roll at Night, 1941
The Maltese Falcon, 1941
All Through the Night, 1942
The Big Shot, 1942
Across the Pacific, 1942
Casablanca, 1943
Action in the North Atlantic, 1943
Thank Your Lucky Stars, 1943
Sahara, 1943
Passage to Marseille, 1944
To Have and Have Not, 1945

Conflict, 1945
Two Guys From Milwaukee, 1946
The Big Sleep, 1946
Dead Reckoning, 1947
The Two Mrs. Carrolls, 1947
Dark Passage, 1947
Always Together, 1948
The Treasure of the Sierra Madre, 1948
Key Largo, 1948
Knock on Any Door, 1949
Tokyo Joe, 1949
Chain Lightning, 1950
In a Lonely Place, 1950
The Enforcer, 1951
Sirocco, 1951
The African Queen, 1951
Deadline-U.S.A., 1952
Battle Circus, 1953
Beat the Devil, 1954
The Caine Mutiny, 1954
Sabrina, 1954
The Barefoot Contessa, 1954
We're No Angels, 1955
The Left Hand of God, 1955
The Desperate Hours, 1955
The Harder They Fall, 1956

Bette Davis
Actress

Real name: Ruth Elizabeth Davis; Born: April 5, 1908
Academy Awards: Best Actress, Dangerous, Jezebel

"What a dump!" Bette Davis complained of the house she shared with Joseph Cotten in *Beyond the Forest.* "I hope you die soon. I'll be waiting for you to die," she encouraged her husband in *The Little Foxes.* "Fasten your seat belts. It's going to be a bumpy night," the actress with a capital "A" cautioned in *All About Eve.* Davis's bitchy monsters said and did terrible things as a means of preserving their rights. In a world dominated by men, confrontation was the "scenery chewer's" stock in trade, and the consequences of loneliness or betrayal were not too high a price to pay.

In her mesmerizing, theatrical style, the actress submerged herself in her characters. She stared down opponents with those bulging Bette Davis eyes. She puffed cigarette smoke and shot furious sentences out of her scarlet mouth as she sashayed about in a get-out-of-my-way manner.

Davis's court battle with Warner Brothers for meatier roles reinforced her movie heroines' message. More threatening than mere feminism, it demanded that one's identity, regardless of gender, comes from work and not from one's spouse, children, parents, or employers. "I've always enjoyed a good honest fight," the spitfire said. Her husbands, most of whom were weaker than she, complained that Davis neglected them for her career. "I never seem to bring out the best in men," was her point of view.

In the 1970s, the actress was honored by a televised American Film Institute Life Achievement award and embarked on a world-wide lecture tour featuring flim clips and a question-and-answer session. In Australia, a fan asked if the wig she was wearing was her real hair. "Yes, it is," she fibbed, without missing a beat, "and these are my real teeth, and my real tits." Asked what she wanted to be remembered as, Bette Davis replied emphatically, "A good worker."

BELOW: This picture of the actress was taken by her mother, Ruth Davis. Of "Ruthie," Davis remarked, "She, it is true, wanted to be an actress. But she would never have made it. I had to be the monster for both of us."

OPPOSITE: A portrait of Davis in her most famous role—the caustic stage actress Margo Channing in *All About Eve.*

OPPOSITE: Davis rose above the script of *Jezebel* and made a defiant southern belle out of Julie Marsden, a role considered compensation for her not getting the part of Scarlett O'Hara in *Gone With the Wind*.

RIGHT: The actress fought with Warner Brothers to play the sluttish, Cockney waitress Mildred in *Of Human Bondage*. "I was disgustingly good," said Davis, who prepared for the role by studying for weeks with a speech teacher to perfect a Cockney accent.

BELOW: Davis with Anne Baxter, Marilyn Monroe, and George Sanders in *All About Eve*, in which she brought out her arsenal of theatrical mannerisms as the temperamental and insecure actress Margo Channing, who worried about getting older.

Bad Sister, 1931
Seed, 1931
Waterloo Bridge, 1931
Way Back Home, 1932
The Menace, 1932
Hell's House, 1932
The Man Who Played God, 1932
So Big, 1932
The Rich Are Always With Us, 1932
The Dark Horse, 1932
Cabin in the Cotton, 1932
Three on a Match, 1932
20,000 Years in Sing Sing, 1933
Parachute Jumper, 1933
The Working Man, 1933
Ex-Lady, 1933
Bureau of Missing Persons, 1933
Fashions of 1934, 1934
The Big Shakedown, 1934
Jimmy the Gent, 1934
Fog Over Frisco, 1934
Of Human Bondage, 1934
Housewife, 1934
Bordertown, 1935
The Girl From Tenth Avenue, 1935
Front Page Woman, 1935
Special Agent, 1935
Dangerous, 1935
The Petrified Forest, 1936
The Golden Arrow, 1936

Satan Met a Lady, 1936
Marked Woman, 1937
Kid Galahad, 1937
That Certain Woman, 1937
It's Love I'm After, 1937
Jezebel, 1938
The Sisters, 1938
Dark Victory, 1939
Juarez, 1939
The Old Maid, 1939
The Private Lives of Elizabeth and
    Essex, 1939
All This and Heaven Too, 1940
The Letter, 1940
The Great Lie, 1941
The Bride Came C.O.D., 1941
The Little Foxes, 1941
The Man Who Came to Dinner, 1941
In This Our Life, 1942
Now, Voyager, 1942
Watch on the Rhine, 1943
Thank Your Lucky Stars, 1943
Old Acquaintance, 1943
Mr. Skeffington, 1944
Hollywood Canteen, 1944
The Corn Is Green, 1945
A Stolen Life, 1946
Deception, 1946
Winter Meeting, 1948
June Bride, 1948

Beyond the Forest, 1949
All About Eve, 1950
Payment on Demand, 1951
Another Man's Poison, 1951
Phone Call From a Stranger, 1952
The Star, 1953
The Virgin Queen, 1955
Storm Center, 1956
The Catered Affair, 1956
John Paul Jones, 1959
The Scapegoat, 1959
Pocketful of Miracles, 1961
What Ever Happened to Baby Jane?,
    1962
The Empty Canvas, 1964
Dead Ringer, 1964
Where Love Has Gone, 1964
Hush . . . Hush, Sweet Charlotte,
    1965
The Nanny, 1965
The Anniversary, 1968
Bunny O'Hare, 1971
Connecting Rooms, 1972
Madame Sin, 1972
The Scientific Cardplayer, 1972
Burnt Offerings, 1976
Return From Witch Mountain,
    1978
Death on the Nile, 1978
The Watcher in the Woods, 1980

LEFT: As a demented former child star in *What Ever Happened to Baby Jane?*, Davis smacked her crippled sister, Joan Crawford, an ex-movie queen. The campy melodrama commenced both superstars' horror-movie cycle of crazy-old-lady roles.

OPPOSITE: For the part of the lonely, vicious, carping Queen Elizabeth I in *The Virgin Queen*, Davis shaved her hairline three inches and removed her eyebrows for authenticity. The actress identified with the complex sovereign but deferred to her "power to roll heads—this she had over me."

Cary Grant Leading Man

Real name: Archibald Alexander Leach; Born: January 18, 1904
Academy Award: Special Oscar "for his unique mastery of the art of screen acting with the respect and
affection of his colleagues"

The suave ladies' man with the clipped British accent, Cary Grant is the movie star everyone hopes will live forever. A solid romantic actor with an exceptional gift for drawing-room and suspense comedy, he brought out the sensuality in his leading ladies (Mae West, Katharine Hepburn, Rita Hayworth, Irene Dunne, and Grace Kelly) by letting them pursue him. A carefree movie bachelor, the available and charming leading man was not an irresponsible one.

As he got older and better looking, the chemistry between the movie camera and the actor—who maintained a year-round suntan to avoid wearing makeup—improved. Because his incredible features allowed him to age with dignity, Grant has never been reduced to parodying his screen persona, the way some movie superstars have had to. Not entirely unblemished, his one minor physical imperfection is being slightly bow-legged. Although his occasionally cavalier screen attitude toward women (one never believed Grant was a hundred percent sincere) predated that of secret agent James (007) Bond, he could always be relied on for dapper polish and lack of pretension.

Not all has been perfect in Grant's life. Four of his five wives left him. "They got bored with me," he says. "I made the mistake of thinking each of my wives was my mother." The pain of being rejected plunged him into depression. In the 1960s, he underwent supervised sessions with the chemical LSD, which he claims relaxed him and made him a less selfish person.

Personally, Cary Grant views himself as a confident, modern businessman (his fortune is estimated at $25 million) who worked his way to the top. In glowing health at nearly eighty, he is still sought after for movie appearances.

OPPOSITE: The magnificently handsome Cary Grant in a 1940s publicity photograph highlighting the indelible cleft in his chin.

BELOW: The crop dust chase in Alfred Hitchcock's comedy-suspense thriller *North by Northwest*, in which Grant, an advertising executive, is mistaken for a spy.

ABOVE: In *I'm No Angel*, Grant softened Mae West's predatory style.

LEFT: The attraction of opposites. Katharine Hepburn, a plucky heiress, and Cary Grant, an absent-minded professor, in the daffy *Bringing Up Baby*. The baby of the movie's title was a leopard—one of two in the film.

OPPOSITE: The leading man brought out the natural elegance of Ingrid Bergman in *Indiscreet*, a second-string trifle.

OPPOSITE: With beauty Grace Kelly in *To Catch a Thief.*

ABOVE: Grant and ex-wife Dyan Cannon with their baby, Jennifer. "It's never too late to become a parent," he boasted.

Charisma meets coiffure. Cary Grant welcomes Farrah Fawcett-Majors, one of television's "Charlie's Angels" to Fabergé, the cosmetics empire of which he's a director and roving goodwill ambassador.

This Is the Night, 1932
Sinners in the Sun, 1932
Merrily We Go to Hell, 1932
The Devil and the Deep, 1932
Blonde Venus, 1932
Hot Saturday, 1932
Madame Butterfly, 1932
She Done Him Wrong, 1933
Woman Accused, 1933
The Eagle and the Hawk, 1933
Gambling Ship, 1933
I'm No Angel, 1933
Alice in Wonderland, 1933
Thirty-Day Princess, 1934
Born to Be Bad, 1934
Kiss and Make Up, 1934
Ladies Should Listen, 1934
Enter Madame, 1935
Wings in the Dark, 1935
The Last Outpost, 1935
Sylvia Scarlett, 1936
Big Brown Eyes, 1936
Suzy, 1936
Wedding Present, 1936
Romance and Riches, 1936
When You're in Love, 1937

Topper, 1937
The Toast of New York, 1937
The Awful Truth, 1937
Bringing Up Baby, 1938
Holiday, 1938
Gunga Din, 1939
Only Angels Have Wings, 1939
In Name Only, 1939
His Girl Friday, 1940
My Favorite Wife, 1940
The Howards of Virginia, 1940
The Philadelphia Story, 1940
Penny Serenade, 1941
Suspicion, 1941
The Talk of the Town, 1942
Once Upon a Honeymoon, 1942
Mr. Lucky, 1943
Destination Tokyo, 1944
Once Upon a Time, 1944
None But the Lonely Heart, 1944
Arsenic and Old Lace, 1944
Without Reservations, 1946
Night and Day, 1946
Notorious, 1946
The Bachelor and the Bobby-Soxer, 1947

The Bishop's Wife, 1947
Mr. Blandings Builds His Dream House, 1948
Every Girl Should Be Married, 1948
I Was a Male War Bride, 1949
Crisis, 1950
People Will Talk, 1951
Room for One More, 1952
Monkey Business, 1952
Dream Wife, 1953
To Catch a Thief, 1955
The Pride and the Passion, 1957
An Affair to Remember, 1957
Kiss Them for Me, 1957
Indiscreet, 1958
Houseboat, 1958
North by Northwest, 1959
Operation Petticoat, 1959
The Grass Is Greener, 1961
That Touch of Mink, 1962
Charade, 1963
Father Goose, 1964
Walk, Don't Run, 1966
Elvis—That's the Way It Is, 1970

Katharine Hepburn The One and Only

Real name: Katharine Houghton Hepburn; Born: November 8, 1909
Academy Awards: Best Actress, Morning Glory, Guess Who's Coming to Dinner, The Lion in Winter, On Golden Pond

During a television interview, Barbara Walters inquired of Katharine Hepburn, "You always seem to know the difference between right and wrong. Do you?" The empress of Yankee empiricism replied disapprovingly, "Don't you?" The most admired and enduring of movie super-greats, Hepburn has received twelve Academy Award nominations and four Oscars—more than any other actor or actress. Whether she's playing the rich, arrogant American girl she cornered the market on, a woman disguised as a man, a spinster, or a devoted wife, she's always the strong-minded, forthright lady who speaks the truth, no matter what, lacing it with humor and common sense.

Bossy yes, boring never. "Lose your sense of humor and you might as well cut your throat," she insists in her irritatingly nasal but unforgettable voice. The most accurate tribute to Hepburn's spirit of independence was outlined by director George Cukor, who worked with her in *Little Women, Sylvia Scarlett, The Philadelphia Story,* and *Adam's Rib:* "It's peculiar but the movie audience is hostile to Kate at the start of a picture. By the middle they're usually sympathetic and, by the end, they're rooting for her."

With handsome Cary Grant, Hepburn took lunatic screwball comedy over the limit; with imperturbable Spencer Tracy, she won the battle of the sexes by being an intelligent good sport; and with Humphrey Bogart and Henry Fonda, she crowned their legends with her imperial presence in films that became award-winning classics. Among her female peers, Ginger Rogers may have been *the* queen of dance, Greta Garbo *the femme fatale,* and Bette Davis *the* actress, but Katharine Hepburn, an exasperating perfectionist, was the first free woman in and out of the American cinema. As an admirer observed, "She doesn't need the right stuff; Katharine Hepburn is the right stuff."

OPPOSITE: Audiences identified Katharine Hepburn with Tracy Lord, the spoiled socialite who gets her comeuppance in *The Philadelphia Story.*

BELOW: Hepburn won a third Oscar for best actress as Eleanor of Aquitaine in *The Lion in Winter.* Constantly battling with her husband, Henry II, and their sons for political power, she stole scenes with lines like, "Hush, dear, mother's fighting," and "Well, what family doesn't have its ups and downs."

OPPOSITE PAGE

TOP LEFT: In a sensational debut, Hepburn played John Barrymore's daughter in *A Bill of Divorcement*.

TOP RIGHT: Star-struck ingenues Ginger Rogers and Katharine Hepburn clash as roommates in *Stage Door*. When Hepburn moves in with a mountain of luggage, Rogers proposes, "Why don't we just sleep in the hall? No sense crowding the trunks."

BOTTOM: Hepburn and the men in Tracy Lord's life: Cary Grant, Jimmy Stewart, and John Howard. The actress bought the movie rights to *The Philadelphia Story*, the Philip Barry comedy she starred in on Broadway.

ABOVE: Henry Fonda and Katharine Hepburn won Oscars for their Norman and Ethel Thayer in *On Golden Pond*.

A Bill of Divorcement, 1932
Christopher Strong, 1933
Morning Glory, 1933
Little Women, 1933
Spitfire, 1934
The Little Minister, 1934
Break of Hearts, 1935
Alice Adams, 1935
Sylvia Scarlett, 1936
Mary of Scotland, 1936
A Woman Rebels, 1936
Quality Street, 1937
Stage Door, 1937
Bringing Up Baby, 1938
Holiday, 1938
The Philadelphia Story, 1940
Stage Door Canteen, 1943

Dragon Seed, 1944
Undercurrent, 1946
Song of Love, 1947
The African Queen, 1951
Summertime, 1955
The Rainmaker, 1956
The Iron Petticoat, 1956
Suddenly, Last Summer, 1959
Long Day's Journey Into Night, 1962
The Lion in Winter, 1968
The Madwoman of Chaillot, 1969
The Trojan Women, 1971
A Delicate Balance, 1973
Rooster Cogburn, 1975
Olly, Olly, Oxen Free, 1981
On Golden Pond, 1981

For Hepburn's Films with Spencer Tracy, see page 120

Spencer Tracy
The Natural

Real name: Spencer Bonaventure Tracy; Born: April 5, 1900; Died: June 11, 1967
Academy Awards: Best Actor, Captains Courageous, Boys Town

Regarded as the movie actor's actor, Spencer Tracy publicly denied there was any mystique to his profession and had no patience with questions about the art of movie acting. "Learn your lines," was his advice to young actors. His performances, highly esteemed for their inspired, less-is-more style, were the result of keeping his acting simple and without affectation. As English actor Sir Laurence Olivier complimented, "There is great truth in everything Spencer Tracy does."

In *State of the Union*, Angela Lansbury pigeonholed Tracy, a businessman her party wants to run for president of the United States: "He's got idealism in one eye and ambition in the other." Off camera, Hollywood's father figure was humble one moment

and belligerent the next. His style of naturalism meant being true to himself even when he contradicted himself. A controversial man, he rebelled against studio warnings that he drank too much with his buddy Pat O'Brien, played reckless polo, and got involved with leading ladies like Loretta Young. In spite of his long relationship with co-star Katharine Hepburn, Tracy, a Catholic, remained married until his death to Louise Treadwell, an actress he met in summer stock.

One of the few actors to come to maturity in front of the movie camera, Tracy's understatement and faultless timing became the hallmarks of naturalistic film acting. He never required motivation, just a script. Whether he was playing a tough priest, feisty

reporter, crusty fisherman, Notre Dame coach, lawyer, politician, or comic foe to Katharine Hepburn's high-strung smart girl, Tracy was the guy you could depend on to help a woman or friend out of a jam. As his flaming red hair turned snowy white, his image enlarged to include that of a father figure and a just and moral man.

OPPOSITE: Tracy's favorite role was the Portuguese fisherman in *Captains Courageous*. While the studio-made adventure was dull, the emotional bond between Tracy and child actor Freddie Bartholomew remained moving and honest.

BELOW: *The Old Man and the Sea* —Tracy's ultimate "Papa" movie. The hard lines in his face have been described as capable of holding two days of rain.

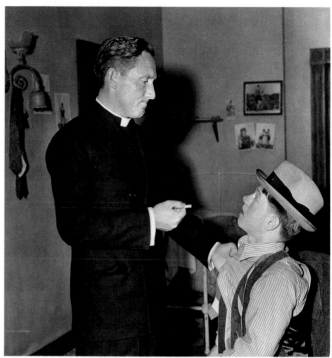

OPPOSITE PAGE

TOP LEFT: In *Father of the Bride*, Tracy, as a typical American dad, spanks daughter, Elizabeth Taylor, for her extravagance and because he's going to lose her.

TOP RIGHT: Spencer Tracy gave the Oscar he won for disciplining Mickey Rooney in *Boys Town* to the real Father Flanagan.

BOTTOM: Tracy as Mayor Frank Skeffington, an old-line politician defeated for re-election in *The Last Hurrah*.

RIGHT: At his funeral, Tracy's estranged wife Louise was escorted by their son John, daughter Susan, and grandson Joseph Spencer Tracy. His son's deafness was said to be a cause of the disintegration of Tracy's marriage. Katharine Hepburn did not attend the services.

Up the River, 1930	It's a Small World, 1935	A Guy Named Joe, 1943
Quick Millions, 1931	The Murder Man, 1935	The Seventh Cross, 1944
Six Cylinder Love, 1931	Dante's Inferno, 1935	Thirty Seconds Over Tokyo, 1944
Goldie, 1931	Whipsaw, 1935	Cass Timberlane, 1947
She Wanted a Millionaire, 1932	Riffraff, 1936	Edward, My Son, 1949
Sky Devils, 1932	Fury, 1936	Malaya, 1950
Disorderly Conduct, 1932	San Francisco, 1936	Father of the Bride, 1950
Young America, 1932	Libeled Lady, 1936	Father's Little Dividend, 1951
Society Girl, 1932	They Gave Him a Gun, 1937	The People Against O'Hara, 1951
Painted Woman, 1932	Captains Courageous, 1937	Plymouth Adventure, 1952
Me and My Gal, 1932	Big City, 1937	The Actress, 1953
20,000 Years in Sing Sing, 1933	Mannequin, 1938	Broken Lance, 1954
Face in the Sky, 1933	Test Pilot, 1938	Bad Day at Black Rock, 1955
Shanghai Madness, 1933	Boys Town, 1938	The Mountain, 1956
The Power and the Glory, 1933	Stanley and Livingstone, 1939	The Old Man and the Sea, 1958
The Mad Game, 1933	I Take This Woman, 1940	The Last Hurrah, 1958
A Man's Castle, 1933	Northwest Passage, 1940	Inherit the Wind, 1960
Looking for Trouble, 1934	Edison, the Man, 1940	The Devil at Four O'Clock, 1961
The Show-Off, 1934	Boom Town, 1940	Judgment at Nuremberg, 1961
Bottoms Up, 1934	Men of Boys Town, 1941	It's a Mad, Mad, Mad, Mad World, 1963
Now I'll Tell, 1934	Dr. Jekyll and Mr. Hyde, 1941	
Marie Galante, 1934	Tortilla Flat, 1942	

For Tracy's films with Katharine Hepburn, see page 120

Spencer Tracy and The Friendly

The Hepburn-Tracy love team symbolized the true meeting of minds in a partnership of respect and shared responsibility. While her films with Spencer Tracy have been labeled "the domestication of Katharine Hepburn," the couple's screen battles concluded in triumphant victories of mutual compromise. Tracy relished outraging Hepburn and she delighted in outsmarting him. An open secret from the start, their twenty-seven-year romance was a tender, intimate, and dignified affair. Though he was always the immovable object to her irresistible force, Hepburn remarked, "I think Spencer and I are the perfect American couple."

Katharine Hepburn
Combatants

The chirpy Hepburn-Tracy comedies and melodramas used funny love stories to make touching points about a professional career woman who's liberated emotionally by a worthy man. In *Adam's Rib* (left) they are married lawyers who argue over everything from the legal system to what to have for breakfast. Tracy prosecutes a messy young housewife played by comedienne Judy Holliday, who is accused of shooting her cheating husband. As the defense attorney, Hepburn gets Holliday acquitted. Establishing female intelligence at the expense of male pride, *Adam's Rib* proved that men and women, though equal, are eternally different.

LEFT: Hepburn and Tracy in *Adam's Rib*, their wittiest comedy, written by Garson Kanin and Ruth Gordon.

BELOW: For *Pat and Mike*, their most physically well-matched bout of comic combustion, Tracy, a sports promoter, manages Hepburn, an amazing athlete who is unbeatable at tennis, golf, and judo. The film contains Tracy's tribute to Hepburn: "There ain't much meat on her but what there is is *cherce*."

Woman of the Year, 1942
Keeper of the Flame, 1942
Without Love, 1945
The Sea of Grass, 1947
State of the Union, 1948
Adam's Rib, 1949
Pat and Mike, 1952
Desk Set, 1957
Guess Who's Coming to Dinner, 1967

For Hepburn's films, see page 113
For Tracy's films, see page 117

ABOVE LEFT: In a serene moment, Spencer Tracy and Katharine Hepburn are captured in *Without Love.*

ABOVE RIGHT: When they met on the set of *Woman of the Year,* their first movie together, Hepburn informed Tracy: "I'm afraid I'm a little tall for you, Mr. Tracy." His retort: "Don't worry, Miss Hepburn, I'll cut you down to my size." In the film, Tracy plays a sports writer and Hepburn a political columnist. They make an unlikely couple, and their marriage almost perishes because of irreconcilable differences. Tracy was impressed with the story about the readjustment of a man and a woman genuinely in love but poles apart in their outlook on life and marriage.

LEFT: Spencer Tracy died ten days after the completion of *Guess Who's Coming to Dinner,* his ninth film with Katharine Hepburn. More memorable than the film's interracial love story between Katharine Houghton (Hepburn's niece) and Sidney Poitier is the scene where Tracy affirms his love for Hepburn: "If what they feel for each other is even half what we felt, then that is everything."

Judy Garland
Singer

Real name: Frances Ethel Gumm; Born: June 10, 1922; Died: June 22, 1969
Academy Award: Special Miniature Oscar "for her outstanding performance as a screen juvenile during the past year (1939)"

The little lady with the great big voice and no formal training was all heart when she sang. With her trusting eyes and fresh-faced, girl-next-door looks, Judy Garland belted out songs in a voice so stunning and overpowering that it made her the first song-and-dance actress to have an impact in movies. A child star in vaudeville, she crooned make-believe love songs at age three. By twelve, she took people's breath away with a torchy version of "My Man." When Garland performed "You Made Me Love You" to Clark Gable's photograph in *Broadway Melody of 1938* and "Over the Rainbow" in *The Wizard of Oz*, the singing sensation became a pop music all-star.

In her teens, Garland developed a weight problem and tried to control it with pills. She soared on studio-prescribed "happy pills," making them a lifelong habit in combination with amphetamines and other drugs. No movie plot could compare to the psychodrama of her life. Her ongoing performance as a put-upon victim elicited fanatic loyalty from fans. Victimhood made the singer the center of attention and allowed her to blame her problems on others—her pushy, show-business mother, exploitative studio bosses, and several husbands who found it impossible to satisfy her.

The Garland cult flowered long before her death, nourished by the "soul in agony" sound of her voice in what have been described as "mass group therapy" concerts between films. To partake of her quivering live or recorded renditions of "The Man That Got Away," "Chicago," and "I Can't Give You Anything But Love" was to know that true love would never last. Trying to construct Judy Garland's definition of love is impossible, except to characterize it as a state of "constantly trembling with happiness."

Her final decline began when she was fired from *Valley of the Dolls* and replaced by Susan Hayward. In Ray Bolger's opinion, the singer "just plain wore out." Her death at forty-seven from an accidental overdose of sleeping pills did not come as a shock. As Garland joked, "Somewhere behind every cloud, there's a lot of rain."

BELOW: At a 1960s comeback concert, Garland, America's Piaf, sucked adrenaline from audiences and poured out familiar torch, swing, and up-tempo standards in her tremulous vibrato.

OPPOSITE: Dorothy and Toto on the Bradford Exchange's mail order "Over the Rainbow" plate. Inspired by *The Wizard of Oz*, it sold for $19.95 in 1977 and is currently valued at $212.

LEFT: Judy Garland (everybody's kid sister) and Mickey Rooney (everybody's kid brother) in *Love Finds Andy Hardy*, one of the nine films they teamed in.

BELOW: Jack Haley, the tin woodman, Ray Bolger, the scarecrow, Bert Lahr, the cowardly lion, and Judy Garland, Dorothy, in *The Wizard of Oz*. The musical fairy tale's undying popularity lies in its message that "you can go home again and again."

OPPOSITE PAGE

TOP LEFT: In *Easter Parade*'s "A Couple of Swells" number, Garland was hailed as "the only Astaire partner you looked at when he danced with her."

TOP RIGHT: Judy Garland and Gene Kelly's robust, showmanlike song-and-dance styles complemented each other in *For Me and My Gal*, a corny patriotic musical that combined the themes of World War I and vaudeville.

BOTTOM: In *A Star is Born*, James Mason, a slipping movie idol, discovers Judy Garland, a band singer. As her star rises, his fades, and he walks into the sea and drowns. Considered the zenith of the singer-actress's film career, the dramatic musical showcased the Garland concert-pleasers—"The Man That Got Away" and the eighteen-minute "Born in a Trunk."

124

OPPOSITE: The "Get Happy" number from *Summer Stock*. The singer tried to commit suicide the year the musical was released.

RIGHT: My mother, myself. Judy Garland and daughter Liza Minnelli, her mother's confidante and sometime surrogate parent.

BELOW: Sounding and looking very much like her mother, Liza Minnelli (here in *New York, New York*) has maintained an impressive film, stage, and concert career. Some consider Minnelli the "I Remember Mama" branch of the Garland cult.

Pigskin Parade, 1936
Broadway Melody of 1938, 1937
Thoroughbreds Don't Cry, 1937
Everybody Sing, 1938
Love Finds Andy Hardy, 1938
Listen Darling, 1938
The Wizard of Oz, 1939
Babes in Arms, 1939
Andy Hardy Meets Debutante, 1940
Strike Up the Band, 1940
Little Nellie Kelly, 1940
Ziegfeld Girl, 1941
Life Begins for Andy Hardy, 1941
Babes on Broadway, 1942
For Me and My Gal, 1942
Presenting Lily Mars, 1943
Thousands Cheer, 1943
Girl Crazy, 1943
Meet Me in St. Louis, 1944
The Clock, 1945
The Harvey Girls, 1946
Ziegfeld Follies, 1946
Till the Clouds Roll By, 1946
The Pirate, 1948
Easter Parade, 1948
Words and Music, 1948
In the Good Old Summertime, 1949
Summer Stock, 1950
A Star Is Born, 1954
Pepe, 1960
Judgment at Nuremberg, 1961
Gay Purr-ee, 1962
A Child Is Waiting, 1963
I Could Go On Singing, 1963

John Wayne Cowboy

Real name: Marion Michael Morrison; Born: May 26, 1907; Died: June 11, 1979
Academy Award: Best Actor, True Grit

Cowboy-lawman John Wayne perfected his "fastest gun in the West" legend in scores of westerns. The strong, silent exterminator with the sunbaked leather face, the laconic rolling gait, and gravel-pitched speaking voice stood for the rugged individualist in Hollywood's vision of the old West. By some unexplained divine patriarchal right, he alone was capable of separating the good guys from the bad guys and dividing women into madonnas or whores.

The Duke (a childhood nickname taken from a favorite dog) had every cowboy move down pat—falling from a horse, drawing and firing a gun in a shoot-out, winning a barroom brawl, and riding tall in the saddle with dignity. In his last film, *The Shootist,* the seemingly indestructible cowboy showed how an aging gunman with cancer should face death. A four-pack-a-day cigarette smoker, he temporarily licked "the big C" after an operation in the 1960s and told doctors "to fix it" when he required open heart surgery in the 1970s.

Fans gobbled up big 6'4" John Wayne's shoot-or-fight-it-out confrontation tactics and his meting out of frontier justice. "I have always believed in facing everything directly," said the Duke. He went a giant step further by using his celluloid cowboy to expound his politics, which have been lampooned as "Go West and turn right." His conservative "my country right or wrong" mumbo-jumbo reassured certain silent majorities.

His 1960s film *The Green Berets* was a personal pro-Vietnam War crusade. Movie historians contend Wayne didn't fathom that art outlasts politics. The cowboy-hero's take-charge style took precedence over his political ideology. When people would tell him "everything isn't black and white," the larger-than-movies gunslinger (who had a Congressional medal struck in his honor) would reply, "Why the hell not?"

OPPOSITE: In *Rio Bravo,* the Duke, as Sheriff John T. Chance, had to shoot it out with hired gunfighters so he could get a murderer to the U.S. marshal.

BELOW: In *Red River,* Wayne, a stubborn cattle baron, punches out his foster son, Montgomery Clift.

ABOVE: Henry Fonda and the Duke were U.S. cavalry officers in *Fort Apache*, a military expedition movie with an Indian massacre.

LEFT: As Colonel Davy Crockett in *The Alamo*, the big man in the saddle arrives to help General Sam Houston liberate Texas from the Mexicans. The Wayne-produced horse opera was not a financial success, but it fostered the idea of "better dead than Mexican," which was reinterpreted as "better dead than red."

RIGHT: *Sands of Iwo Jima* was the flag-waving patriot's favorite film because he got to join the Marines. Wayne did not serve in World War II for health reasons.

BELOW: The Duke and third wife, Pilar, with Marissa, Aissa, and John Ethan. Wayne was married three times to beautiful Latin American women and had seven children and numerous grandchildren.

Hangman's House, 1928
Words and Music, 1929
Salute, 1929
Men Without Women, 1930
Rough Romance, 1930
Cheer Up and Smile, 1930
The Big Trail, 1930
Girls Demand Excitement, 1931
Three Girls Lost, 1931
Men Are Like That (a.k.a. Arizona), 1931
Range Feud, 1931
The Deceiver, 1931
Maker of Men, 1931
Shadow of the Eagle, 1932
Texas Cyclone, 1932
Two Fisted Law, 1932
Lady and Gent, 1932
Hurricane Express, 1932
Ride Him Cowboy, 1932
The Big Stampede, 1932
Haunted Gold, 1932
The Telegraph Trail, 1933
The Three Musketeers, 1933
Central Airport, 1933
Somewhere in Sonara, 1933
His Private Secretary, 1933
The Life of Jimmy Dolan, 1933
Baby Face, 1933
The Man From Monterey, 1933
Riders of Destiny, 1933
College Coach, 1933
Sagebrush Trail, 1933
Lucky Texan, 1934
West of the Divide, 1934
Blue Steel, 1934
The Man From Utah, 1934
Randy Rides Alone, 1934
The Star Packer, 1934
The Trail Beyond, 1934
'Neath Arizona Skies, 1934
The Lawless Frontier, 1935
Texas Terror, 1935
Rainbow Valley, 1935
Paradise Canyon, 1935
The Dawn Rider, 1935
Westward Ho, 1935
Desert Trail, 1935
The New Frontier, 1935
The Lawless Range, 1935
The Lawless Nineties, 1936
King of the Pecos, 1936
The Oregon Trail, 1936

Winds of the Wasteland, 1936
The Sea Spoilers, 1936
The Lonely Trail, 1936
Conflict, 1936
California Straight Ahead, 1937
I Cover the War, 1937
Idol of the Crowds, 1937
Adventure's End, 1937
Born to the West (a.k.a. Hell Town), 1938
Pals of the Saddle, 1938
Overland Stage Raiders, 1938
Santa Fe Stampede, 1938
Red River Range, 1938
Stagecoach, 1939
The Night Riders, 1939
Three Texas Steers, 1939
Wyoming Outlaw, 1939
New Frontier, 1939
Allegheny Uprising, 1939
Dark Command, 1940
Three Faces West, 1940
The Long Voyage Home, 1940
Seven Sinners, 1940
A Man Betrayed, 1941
Lady From Louisiana, 1941
The Shepherd of the Hills, 1941
Lady for a Night, 1941
Reap the Wild Wind, 1942
The Spoilers, 1942
In Old California, 1942
Flying Tigers, 1942
Reunion in France, 1942
Pittsburgh, 1942
A Lady Takes a Chance, 1943
In Old Oklahoma, 1943
The Fighting Seabees, 1944
Tall in the Saddle, 1944
Flame of the Barbary Coast, 1945
Back to Bataan, 1945
Dakota, 1945
They Were Expendable, 1945
Without Reservations, 1946
Angel and the Badman, 1947
Tycoon, 1947
Fort Apache, 1948
Red River, 1948
Three Godfathers, 1948
Wake of the Red Witch, 1949
The Fighting Kentuckian, 1949
She Wore a Yellow Ribbon, 1949
Sands of Iwo Jima, 1949

Rio Grande, 1950
Operation Pacific, 1951
Flying Leathernecks, 1951
The Quiet Man, 1952
Big Jim McLain, 1952
Trouble Along the Way, 1953
Island in the Sky, 1953
Hondo, 1953
The High and the Mighty, 1954
The Sea Chase, 1955
Blood Alley, 1955
The Conqueror, 1956
The Searchers, 1956
The Wings of Eagles, 1957
Jet Pilot, 1957
Legend of the Lost, 1957
I Married a Woman, 1958
The Barbarian and the Geisha, 1958
Rio Bravo, 1959
The Horse Soldiers, 1959
The Alamo, 1960
North to Alaska, 1960
The Comancheros, 1961
The Man Who Shot Liberty Valance, 1962
Hatari!, 1962
The Longest Day, 1962
How the West Was Won, 1962
Donovan's Reef, 1963
McLintock, 1963
Circus World, 1964
The Greatest Story Ever Told, 1965
In Harm's Way, 1965
The Sons of Katie Elder, 1965
Cast a Giant Shadow, 1966
The War Wagon, 1967
El Dorado, 1967
The Green Berets, 1968
Hellfighters, 1969
True Grit, 1969
The Undefeated, 1969
Chisum, 1970
Rio Lobo, 1970
Big Jake, 1971
The Cowboys, 1972
Cancel My Reservation, 1972
The Train Robbers, 1973
Cahill, United States Marshal, 1973
McQ, 1974
Brannigan, 1975
Rooster Cogburn, 1975
The Shootist, 1976

OPPOSITE: As the hardbitten, one-eyed marshal Rooster Cogburn in *True Grit*.

Pop artifact: The John Wayne Great American button.

Elizabeth Taylor
Love Goddess

Real name: Elizabeth Rosemond Taylor; Born: February 27, 1932
Academy Awards: Best Actress, Butterfield 8, Who's Afraid of Virginia Woolf?

The last of the breed, Elizabeth Taylor is Hollywood's only true love goddess. She represents all of us who, at one time in our lives, have loved someone more than we love ourselves and will do anything to get that person. This condition has been the motivation for her memorable and excruciating film performances as well as her marriages and divorces.

The very pretty child with deep violet-colored eyes and star quality grew up to be one of the world's most beautiful-but-unconcerned-with-her-looks women. After *National Velvet* and *Courage of Lassie*, Taylor traded in horses and dogs for men in *A Place in the Sun* and *Cat on a Hot Tin Roof*. Her avocation, however, was and is falling in and out of love on magazine covers and surviving serious illnesses in newspaper headlines.

Fans don't envy the star's jewels, wealth, or tragedies as much as they worship her refusal to relinquish the hope of finding a great and lasting love with one man. Never mind that the kind of love the movie magazine queen yearns for may not exist—her aim is true. Her method of entrapment is best summarized as "I need you to take care of me and in return I will be whomever you want me to be."

After wrecking Debbie Reynolds and Eddie Fisher's marriage and recovering from pneumonia and a tracheotomy, which left a scar on her throat, Taylor got Fisher and the public's sympathy when she picked up her Oscar for Gloria Wandrous in *Butterfield 8*. In Taylor's opinion, Wandrous was "the slut of all times" until she found love in the movie with a married socialite, Laurence Harvey.

Enter Richard Burton and the making of *Cleopatra*. Exit fourth husband Eddie Fisher. With the exception of *Who's Afraid of Virginia Woolf?*, the Taylor-Burton films are considered to be a limp series of variations on their up-and-down relationship. Though the world felt they were made for each other, the couple married and divorced twice. True to form, the love goddess then married and separated from seventh husband Senator John Warner, the man she said she wanted "to be buried with."

BELOW: The fourteen-year-old beauty with Donald Crisp in *National Velvet*.

OPPOSITE: In *Butterfield 8*, Taylor as the part-time model and call girl Gloria Wandrous.

ELIZABETH TAYLOR M-G-M

TOP LEFT: Taylor's career as a dramatic actress began in *A Place in the Sun* with Montgomery Clift.

TOP RIGHT: "I feel like a cat on a hot tin roof," screeched Taylor in *Cat on a Hot Tin Roof* with Paul Newman.

BOTTOM: The Todds with good friends Debbie Reynolds and Eddie Fisher. "I have given him my eternal love," Elizabeth Taylor said of third husband Mike Todd, the flamboyant showman who died in a plane crash.

ABOVE: The furor of publicity over the Taylor-Burton romance on the set of *Cleopatra* didn't prevent the movie from being one of Hollywood's most expensive flops.

RIGHT: Before their first marriage, the lovers gave a one-performance-only poetry reading, "World Enough and Time."

FAR RIGHT: After her fling with a car salesman and his with a model, the Burtons remarried in a mud hut village in Africa.

There's One Born Every Minute, 1942
Lassie Come Home, 1943
Jane Eyre, 1944
The White Cliffs of Dover, 1944
National Velvet, 1944
Courage of Lassie, 1946
Cynthia, 1947
Life With Father, 1947
A Date With Judy, 1948
Julia Misbehaves, 1948
Little Women, 1949
Conspirator, 1950
The Big Hangover, 1950
Father of the Bride, 1950
Quo Vadis, 1951
Father's Little Dividend, 1951
A Place in the Sun, 1951
Callaway Went Thataway, 1951
Love Is Better Than Ever, 1952
Ivanhoe, 1952
The Girl Who Had Everything, 1953
Rhapsody, 1954
Elephant Walk, 1954
Beau Brummel, 1954
The Last Time I Saw Paris, 1954
Giant, 1956
Raintree County, 1957
Cat on a Hot Tin Roof, 1958
Suddenly, Last Summer, 1959
Scent of Mystery, 1960
Butterfield 8, 1960
Cleopatra, 1963
The V.I.P.s, 1965
The Sandpiper, 1965
Who's Afraid of Virginia Woolf?, 1966
The Taming of the Shrew, 1967
Reflections in a Golden Eye, 1967
The Comedians, 1967
Doctor Faustus, 1968
Boom!, 1968
Secret Ceremony, 1969
The Only Game in Town, 1970
Under Milk Wood, 1971
X Y & Zee, 1972
Hammersmith Is Out, 1972
Night Watch, 1973
Ash Wednesday, 1973
That's Entertainment, 1974
The Driver's Seat, 1975
The Blue Bird, 1976
A Little Night Music, 1977
Winter Kills, 1979
The Mirror Crack'd, 1980

In their one critical triumph, *Who's Afraid of Virginia Woolf?*, Liz and Dick played "humiliate the host" and "get the guests" with Sandy Dennis and George Segal. Taylor was dynamic as a bitchy college president's daughter married to a mediocre professor, played by Burton with consummate discipline.

RIGHT TOP : The on-again, off-again couple on the cover of *People* magazine. In the 1980s Taylor and Burton made their first Broadway appearance together in a revival of Noel Coward's comedy *Private Lives*, about a witty divorced couple who meet again when each is honeymooning with someone else.

RIGHT: The magazine cover champ posed in some of her jewels, including the Peregina pearl, for *Life*'s tribute.

James Dean
Rebel

Real name: James Byron Dean; Born: February 8, 1931; Died: September 30, 1955

His death at twenty-four in a sports car crash made James Dean the irreplaceable screen rebel. While his 1950s rebellion against a hypocritical society, middle-class values, and tyrannical parents seems silly in comparison to 1980s nuclear arms protests, the pain and frustration Dean projected in putting his program across remain in vogue. The rebel's neoteric pout, the distant helpless look in his eyes (caused by poor eyesight), the slinky, macho, male-model way he wore tight jeans, and the little-boy sneer on his chiseled face have never been duplicated.

When it came to "attitude," James Dean had it all over would-be rebels Montgomery Clift, Paul Newman, and Steve McQueen. His biggest drawing card was portraying crazy mixed-up delinquents groping for love. Uncommunicative and idiosyncratic, he embodied youth culture by combining the teenage fantasies of getting away with rebellion while getting rich from it at the same time.

In his brief life Dean was made miserable by the death of his mother. "My mother died on me when I was nine years old. What does she expect me to do? Do it all by myself?" he agonized. Though he could never forgive her loss, it was knowing that he would never have the love of his father, with whom he had a troubled relationship, that crucified him. The support, love, and discipline he begged for from his movie fathers in *East of Eden* and *Rebel Without a Cause* convinced audiences of his terrible unhappiness.

Nicholas Ray, director of *Rebel Without a Cause*, believed Dean would have surpassed any actor alive because of his inventive capacity to reach the intricate depths beneath a character's surface. Others believed that if Dean had been born twenty years later, he would have found fulfillment as a rock megastar. Unstable and brooding, the rebel was an adventurer always open to new and dangerous experiences, including bisexuality and race car driving. After meeting him, Marlon Brando purportedly commented, "I met a guy at a party last night and I saw myself. But he's doomed."

OPPOSITE: In *Rebel Without a Cause*, the sinuous Dean, who is unimaginable as an adult, hypnotized teenagers in his red jacket with its symbolic message of rage and blood.

BELOW: Dean plays the bongos at a drum lesson with Cyril Jackson in a studio near Times Square.

OPPOSITE PAGE

TOP: *Rebel Without a Cause*'s ill-fated trio. Sal Mineo hero-worshiped James Dean, and Natalie Wood had a crush on him. Mineo was stabbed to death in a Sunset Blvd. parking lot, and Wood slipped off a yacht and drowned.

BOTTOM: In *East of Eden* with Julie Harris. Rejected by his father, Dean sets out to find his mother, the madam of a whorehouse.

ABOVE LEFT: The rebel in a race car.

ABOVE RIGHT: Dean's head was almost severed from his body when he crashed his silver-grey Porsche Spyder on the way to a race.

RIGHT: The French poster for *East of Eden* venerates Dean's gone but not forgotten rebel with an invisible chip on both shoulders.

JAMES DEAN

A L'EST D'EDEN

UN FILM D'ELIA KAZAN

WARNER BROS
A Warner Communications Company présente
Un film d'ELIA KAZAN
A L'EST D'EDEN
D'après le roman de JOHN STEINBECK
avec JULIE HARRIS...JAMES DEAN...RAYMOND MASSEY
et BURL IVES . CINEMASCOPE / TECHNICOLOR
Musique de LEONARD ROSENMAN . Scénario de Paul Osborn

Sailor Beware, 1951
Fixed Bayonets, 1951
Has Anybody Seen My Gal, 1952
Trouble Along the Way, 1953
East of Eden, 1955
Rebel Without a Cause, 1955
Giant, 1956

The actor's most outstanding performance was as Jett Rink, the surly ranch hand who strikes it rich in *Giant*. This shot of Elizabeth Taylor and James Dean in his rebel-martyr crucifixion pose was not used in the movie. Before his death, the egotistical Dean pondered the meaning of life, death, and immortality: "If a man can bridge the gap between life and death, if he can live after he's died, then maybe he was a great man. Immortality is the only true success."

Marilyn Monroe
Sex Symbol

Real name: Norma Jean Mortenson (a.k.a. Norma Jean Baker)
Born: June 1, 1926; Died: August 5, 1962

She is the unrivaled "living-dead" movie star. The anything-goes platinum girl, Saint Marilyn of sex, sleeping pills, and champagne was every fantasy blonde who had ever been in the movies—but with a difference. "MM" was the only Hollywood sex symbol (5 feet 2½ inches tall, 118 pounds, 37-inch bust, 24-inch waist, 37-inch hips) who had "flesh impact" because of the way her coloring, bone structure, and flesh tones struck film. On screen and in photographs you could almost touch her marshmallow skin. Her moist, candy-colored mouth, voluptuous pop-up breasts, and protruding derrière promised she was always ready for sex. She was also a natural at projecting the movie acting technique of "it's not what you do but the look on your face when you do it."

A terrific comedienne, Monroe was funny as long as she parodied herself as the dumb blonde. The joke is always on her in *Bus Stop*, *The Seven Year Itch*, and *Some Like It Hot*, and the humor is often sad, not stomach-clutchingly funny. Because of her death at thirty-six from an overdose of barbiturates, it will never be known if the sex symbol had the stamina and ability to become the outstanding serious actress she claimed she wanted to be.

Whether she committed "accidental suicide" (she held rehearsals for it) or was possibly murdered, death was her salvation. A fatherless child who had a history of insanity on her mother's side of the family, Monroe was constantly in search of who she might really be. Success, money, and praise could not compensate the neurotic movie goddess for being an orphan. In her drug-poisoned mind, reality meant everyone and everything had to let her down eventually. (She slept in a brassiere because she was afraid of her breasts sagging.)

Eulogized as the godmother of the 1960s sexual revolution, the mythic sex symbol achieved in death the identity she longed for in life. Like certain presidents and composers, Marilyn Monroe has the distinction of being the only movie superstar whose death is commemorated once, if not twice, a decade in a blitz of books, magazines, plays, and TV movies.

BELOW: "Sure I posed. I was hungry," said Monroe of the nude-on-red velvet pin-up shot she was paid fifty dollars to do. Photographer Tom Kelley was proud of the picture's composition because it was symmetrical no matter which way the photograph was turned.

OPPOSITE: Monroe as the confused and lost Cherie in *Bus Stop*.

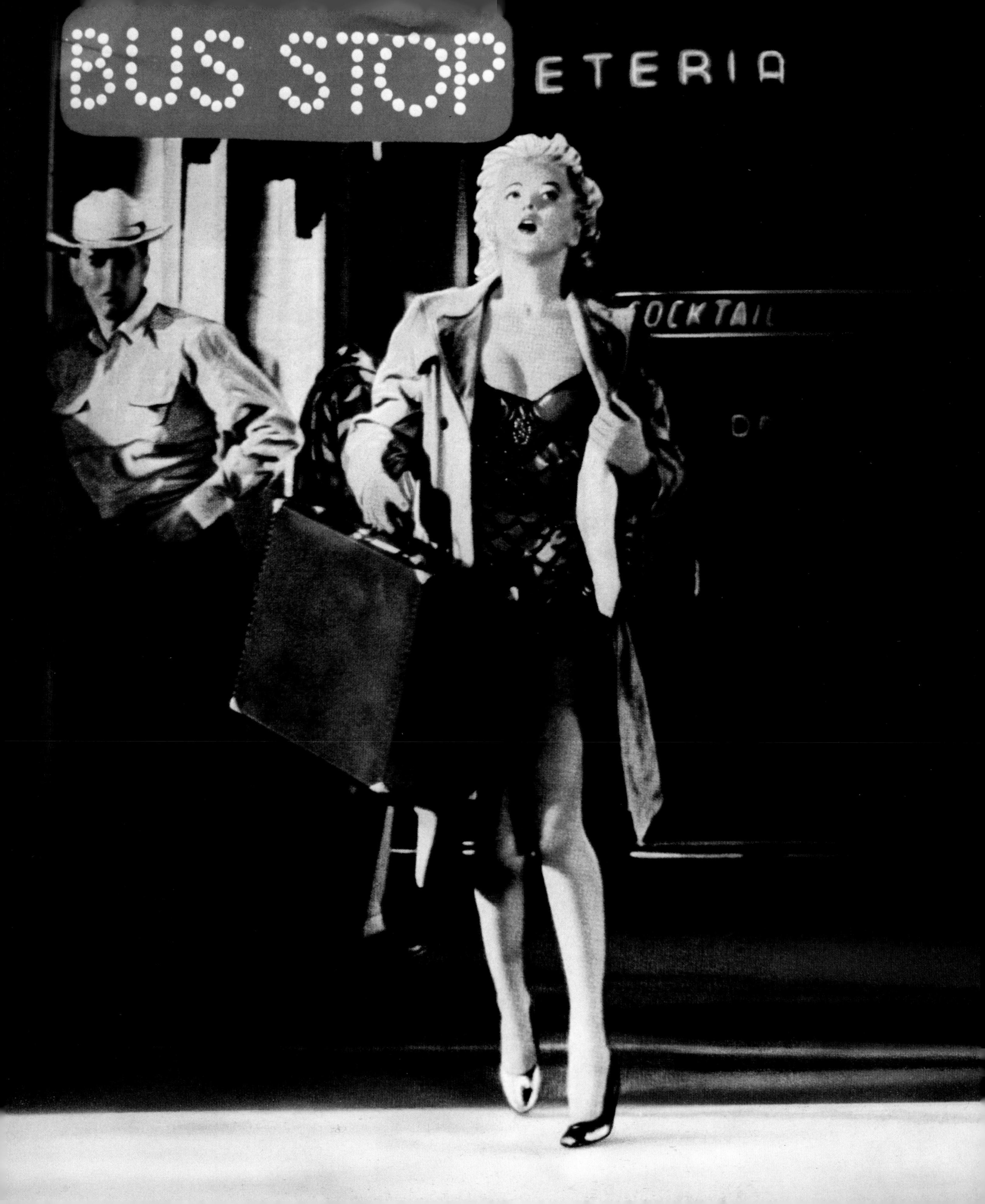
BUS STOP
ETERIA
OCKTAIL

OPPOSITE LEFT: Monroe and Jane Russell grind in *Gentlemen Prefer Blondes*.

OPPOSITE TOP: In *Some Like It Hot*, "MM" cures Tony Curtis's fake impotence.

OPPOSITE BOTTOM: With her imaginary father, Clark Gable, in *The Misfits*.

LEFT TOP: Second husband Joe DiMaggio and the great American body.

LEFT BOTTOM: Marilyn Monroe sang "Happy Birthday" to President John F. Kennedy at Madison Square Garden.

BELOW: Monroe on a subway grating during production of *The Seven Year Itch*.

OVERLEAF: On assignment for *Vogue*, Bert Stern photographed Monroe shortly before her death. Stern's goal, as he wrote in his book *The Last Sitting*, was "to get Marilyn Monroe alone in a room, with no one else around, and take all her clothes off." At his suggestion she wrapped herself in a sheet. . . . It slipped away. After the final photo session, a *Vogue* editor commented, "What's going to happen to that poor girl?"

Marlon Brando Nonconformist

Real name: Marlon Brando, Jr.; Born: April 3, 1924
Academy Awards: Best Actor, On the Waterfront, The Godfather

The appearance of Marlon Brando, the ultimate 1950s anti-hero in jeans and T-shirt, mangled what remained of old-fashioned Hollywood glamour. Unparalleled for his public and cinematic mumblings, moodiness, unpredictability, and bursts of anger, the most influential of all film actors is bound to his definition of nonconformity. For over thirty years he has pontificated: "I just want to be normally insane." "I don't believe in awards of any kind." "I agree that no man is an island, but I also feel that conformity breeds mediocrity."

After the breakthrough performances in *A Streetcar Named Desire, The Wild One,* and *On the Waterfront,* critics complained that Brando wasted his talent in a string of idiotic movies for money. But the nonconformist has redeemed himself with daring and emotionally complicated perform-ances in *Burn!, The Godfather, Last Tango in Paris,* and *Apocalypse Now.*

The unrestrainable Brando despises interviews ("My private life is my own business."). He deprecates acting, which he doesn't seem to enjoy as "dull, boring, childish work." He laments his tempestuous relationships with exotic dark-skinned women as the fault of his own sexual guilt, and he regrets his inability to trust or to love anyone completely. Yet he's always being touted as a gentle person and loving father.

Brando scrutinizes his own pretensions as brutally as those of others. "As soon as you become an actor, people start asking you questions about politics, astrology, archeology, and birth control. What's even funnier, you start giving opinions," he chides. At odds with himself, he's notorious for his dislike of phonies. Perhaps, as has been suggested, "Marlon Brando is the biggest phony of all."

But the restless loner cannot be accused of avoiding risks or imaginative departures in his acting. Whether he blows up to a 300-pound slob or stuffs his cheeks for a haunting performance as Don Corleone in *The Godfather,* Brando exercises a fascination on the public by never vacillating from his image as the supercilious leader of a pack with one charter member.

BELOW: An overweight Brando appeared in Francis Ford Coppola's anti-war film *Apocalypse Now* because he sympathized with the director's views on the horrors of war.

OPPOSITE: Asked in *The Wild One* what he's rebelling against, Johnny, the motorcycle gang leader with the truculent smirk, muttered, "What have you got?"

The Men, 1950
A Streetcar Named Desire, 1951
Viva Zapata!, 1952
Julius Caesar, 1953
The Wild One, 1953
On the Waterfront, 1954
Désirée, 1954
Guys and Dolls, 1955
The Teahouse of the August Moon, 1956
Sayonara, 1957
The Young Lions, 1958
The Fugitive Kind, 1960
One-Eyed Jacks, 1961
Mutiny on the Bounty, 1962
The Ugly American, 1962
Bedtime Story, 1964
Morituri, 1965
The Chase, 1966
The Appaloosa, 1966
The Countess from Hong Kong, 1967
Reflections in a Golden Eye, 1967
Candy, 1968
The Night of the Following Day, 1969
Burn!, 1970
The Nightcomers, 1972
The Godfather, 1972
Last Tango in Paris, 1972
The Missouri Breaks, 1976
Superman, 1978
Apocalypse Now, 1979
The Formula, 1980

OPPOSITE PAGE

TOP LEFT: As Stanley Kowalski in *A Streetcar Named Desire*, Brando yelled for Stella (Kim Hunter).

TOP RIGHT: With Karl Malden and Eva Marie Saint in *On the Waterfront*. "I could have been a contender. I could have been somebody, instead of a bum, which is what I am," said Brando, who stamped the film with his Method acting.

BOTTOM: More exhibitionistic than the sexual marathon with Maria Schneider in *Last Tango in Paris* was Brando's stream-of-consciousness dialogue about an unhappy childhood, estrangement from parents, and bitter relationships with women.

ABOVE: The concerned Indian civil rights activist with a Wounded Knee survivor at a fundraising dinner.

RIGHT: "The Mafia is so American," insists Brando. He refused to accept the Oscar for best actor as Don Vito ("I'll make him an offer he can't refuse") Corleone in *The Godfather* to protest the plight of American Indians.

OVERLEAF: As the Sicilian orphan who becomes a Mafia emperor, Brando infused the character of Vito Corleone in *The Godfather* with suspicion and compassion.

The New Generation

Barbra Streisand Superstar

Real name: Barbara Joan Streisand; Born: April 24, 1942
Academy Awards: Best Actress, Funny Girl; Best Original Song, "Evergreen," A Star Is Born

Oscar. Emmy. Tony. Grammy. Barbra Streisand, the critic-proof superstar, has won them all. A nimble, natural comedienne, the ugly duckling kook who escaped from Brooklyn (for her "the land of boredom, baseball, and bad breath") has been attacked for being aloof, suspicious, elegant, vulgar, crude, charming, and generous. Multi-talented, overbearing, and fast-talking, she can be the type of person you want to strangle in mid-sentence. But when she wrings a song inside out in her pounding two-octave tessitura, with its soft and low and screechy and surging ranges, she's a wonder.

Streisand is loved and hated as a movie star for one reason—because she invites audiences to join in celebrating her successes. Called temperamental and a "ball breaker," the singer-actress insists on artistic and other controls over her films and singing engagements. "If a man did the same thing," she points out, "he would

be called thorough." People who work with her may not get along with her, but they come away admiring how she fights for her integrity. *For Pete's Sake* director Peter Yates hails Streisand as an unfailing professional. "She has ideas and imagination, and people can't forgive her because quite often she is right."

The American beauty rose with an American beauty nose has always been more of a personality than a performer. When she opened in the Broadway musical *Funny Girl*, she sang out her position, "I'm the greatest star. I am by far." During the filming of *Funny Girl*, Streisand all but took over from veteran director William Wyler. "Give her a chance, this is the first movie she's ever directed," someone on the set said. While making *The Way We Were*, the workaholic Barbra Streisand drove co-star Robert Redford crazy by rehearsing and talking scenes to death before she would film

them. In addition to producing and writing the theme song for her superstar vehicle *A Star Is Born*, she gave ulcers to the crew.

"If you pretend to be someone you are not, you are nothing" is Streisand's *modus operandi*. Obsessive in seeking new movie frontiers to conquer, she directs, sings, and stars in *Yentl*, the film of Isaac Bashevis Singer's story about a Jewish girl who disguises herself as a man in order to become a rabbi and then marries the fiancée of the man she loves.

BELOW: In her remake of *A Star Is Born*, the pop diva on the way up was married to Kris Kristofferson, a destructive rock star on the way out.

OPPOSITE: Profile of the superstar. Barbra Streisand has been compared to women in Modigliani paintings and to Nefertiti, the Egyptian queen.

ABOVE: In *Funny Girl*, the singer-actress re-created the rise to fame and the un-happy marriage of comedienne Fanny Brice, the 1920s Ziegfeld star. The musical comedy was notable for her exhilarating delivery of "People" and "Don't Rain on My Parade."

LEFT: Sought out as a model by the world's greatest photographers, Barbra Streisand poses here for Cecil Beaton.

OPPOSITE: *A Star Is Born*'s bathtub scene, in which Streisand makes up Kris Kristofferson's face. "What is female, what is male?" she questions. "There are no set roles any more. There's no time for them."

ABOVE: Fooling around with husband Elliott Gould in the pool of the Beverly Hills Hotel. When they met, he was the star of Broadway's *I Can Get It for You Wholesale* and she was the secretary, Miss Marmelstein. Their marriage foundered as she became more and more famous.

RIGHT: In *The Way We Were*, Streisand revealed the darker side of Robert Redford's all-American golden boy. She also lived out the fantasy of millions of women with imperfect features who "want to capture a man like him by the force of their personality."

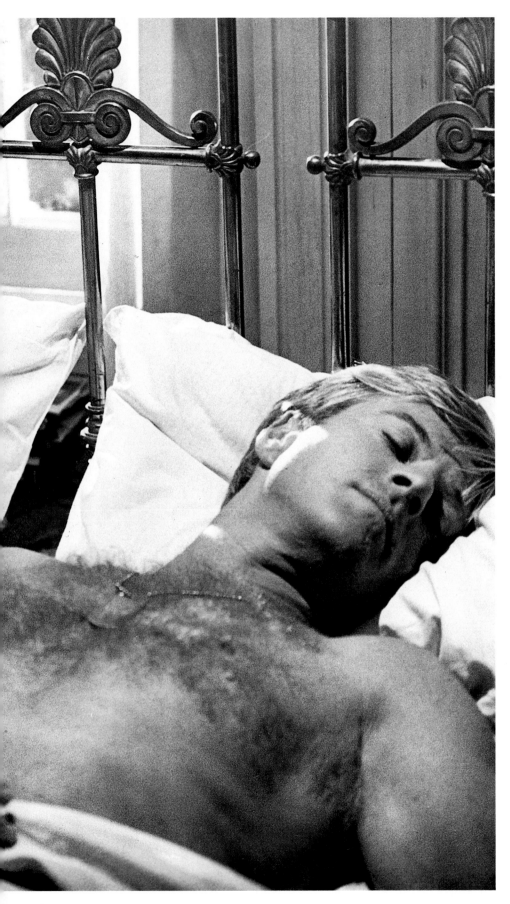

Showing off Golden Globe awards for *A Star Is Born*, Streisand and boyfriend Jon Peters, a hairdresser turned movie producer.

Funny Girl, 1968
Hello, Dolly!, 1969
On a Clear Day You Can See Forever, 1970
The Owl and the Pussycat, 1970
What's Up Doc?, 1972
Up the Sandbox, 1972
The Way We Were, 1973
For Pete's Sake, 1974
Funny Lady, 1975
A Star Is Born, 1976
The Main Event, 1979
All Night Long, 1981
Yentl, 1983

Robert Redford
Winner

Real name: Charles Robert Redford, Jr.; Born: August 18, 1937; Academy Award: Best Director, Ordinary People

Bucking the system and winning his way made Robert Redford the hero and heartthrob of the 1970s. Though the manly and handsome blue-eyed movie god seems too good, too humanistic, and too cause-oriented to be true, he is always irresistible. In his buddy-buddy movies, his man alone series, and his comedies and dramas with strong female partners like Barbra Streisand and Jane Fonda, Redford has gone farther than the good-looking leading men of the past by subjecting his perfect-looking golden boy image to scrutiny. Redford's man is either an independent winner who succeeds by using unorthodox methods or he's a bland, weak, and flawed WASP, like the writer who sells out in *The Way We Were*, the self-centered win-at-all-costs skier in *Downhill Racer*, or the lawyer who becomes an egotistical politician in *The Candidate*.

"Image is crap," denounces Redford, who feels audiences confuse the actor with the role and who resents being labeled as a "pretty face." Accused by some of walking through parts, he is regarded by others as Spencer Tracy's heir because of his ability to be natural and spontaneous in films. Sydney Pollack, who directed him in *The Electric Horseman*, describes Redford's acting as uncerebral, unacademic, purely gut-level. The actor had to be convinced, however, to do the love story *The Way We Were* with Barbra Streisand, which established him as the thinking woman's sex object. As for why he won't make more romantic dramas, Redford says, "Give me a good healthy love story about people who love each other, not some heavy piece of neurosis, and I'll do it."

The movie star-activist has lobbied for solar energy, conservation, and the Equal Rights Amendment. A Redford film never preaches causes but gets them across in an entertaining, decorative fashion. "I'm constantly wrestling with issues as a person, my feelings about America, the environment, and the system. I work out that struggle in film," he says. Making a mid-career switch from acting to directing, Redford won an Oscar for the emotionally intense *Ordinary People* about the undercurrents in the life of a Midwestern family.

OPPOSITE: Redford, an aging rodeo champ, hustled breakfast cereal for a large conglomerate in *The Electric Horseman*.

BELOW: In *The Candidate*, Redford runs for the United States Senate by taking a tough stand on issues. Allowing his media image to be molded by political professionals, he wins at the cost of his principles. "Politics is a bad game and the public always gets ripped off," he says.

TOP: In *Butch Cassidy and the Sundance Kid*, Paul Newman and Robert Redford as the playful outlaws, who joked as they robbed banks and trains.

CENTER: The lovable con artists Redford and Newman pull *The Sting* on Robert Shaw.

BOTTOM: Redford bought the movie rights to *All the President's Men* and cast himself and Dustin Hoffman as journalists Bob Woodward and Carl Bernstein, who investigated the Watergate break-in that led to the resignation of President Richard M. Nixon.

OPPOSITE: In *Jeremiah Johnson*, Redford turns his back on civilization for the life of a mountain man who survives in the wilderness.

LEFT: Redford directs Mary Tyler Moore in the role of a mother who's out of touch with her disturbed teen-age son in the suburban-family drama *Ordinary People.*

BELOW: Radical ethnic clashes with middle-of-the-road WASP. In *The Way We Were,* Barbra Streisand and Robert Redford were a mismatched couple drawn together by her interest in his writing. Their marriage fails because of their differences. He believes people are more important than causes, while she maintains that people are their principles.

OPPOSITE: Conservationists Robert Redford and his wife of almost twenty-five years, Lola Van Wagenen, with their daughter in front of their tri-level, triple-A-frame cedar house in Utah.

Jane Fonda
Protester

Real name: Jane Seymour Fonda; Born: December 21, 1937; Academy Awards: Best Actress, Klute, Coming Home

Depending on whether you wear a "No Nukes" or a "Nuclear Plants Are Better Built Than Jane Fonda" T-shirt, you either adore or abhor the actress and her message movies. The Joan of Arc of fitness, pacifism, and antinuclear proliferation is a fearful presence because of her indisputable claim that we are an overpopulated world doomed by our own pollution. "She can't refrain," says a friend, "from spreading the word and telling the truth, whether it's good or bad and whether you want to hear it or not."

Says the highly publicized and controversial Fonda, whose impassioned acting has been subordinated to her messianic image, "I don't care about the Oscar. I make movies to support the causes I believe in." Movie producer, feminist, and champion of the masses, the well-groomed multimillionaire lives a middle-class life in Santa Monica with her two children and husband, political activist Tom Hayden. The couple share childcare and household chores.

Fonda achieved recognition in movies when she switched from saucy sextoy roles to those of socially and politically committed women in *Klute*, *Coming Home*, and *The China Syndrome*. "I felt lonely a lot for the first thirty years of my life," she says. "I began to work in a political way. I may have lost a reputation and a lot of friends, but essentially what I lost was cynicism. I moved from my sex kitten image because I found hope."

The major influence in her life was her father. "He had power," says the actress. "I became my father's son. I was going to make him love me, to be tough and strong." Her mother, one of Henry Fonda's five wives, committed suicide when Jane Fonda was twelve. It wasn't until years later that she and her father, who opposed her anti-Establishment causes, were completely reconciled.

One of the world's best-looking women, the protester, who's in her forties, crusades for proper diet and muscles with the same zeal she expends on politics. Profits from her workout centers and her best seller *Jane Fonda's Workout Book* go to the Campaign for Economic Democracy, a political organization concerned with environmental cancers, abortion rights, and the political programs of her husband.

BELOW: The "exercist" on the cover of her best-selling workout manual.

OPPOSITE: Fonda's hair was dyed "Brenda Starr" red for the part of the television news reporter who witnesses an accident at a nuclear power plant in *The China Syndrome*. The accident at Three Mile Island nuclear power plant occurred shortly after the prophetic film opened.

Fonda with Katharine Hepburn and her father, Henry, in *On Golden Pond*, one of the few movies to explore a troubled and unhappy father-daughter relationship. The film was Jane Fonda's present to her late father. "I'm in awe of her," Henry Fonda told reporters before his death. Said the daughter of her father: "I've learned to love the things that are strange about him, like how he can say things that are warm and intimate to the press about me, but he won't say them to me directly."

Tall Story, 1960
Walk on the Wild Side, 1962
The Chapman Report, 1962
Period of Adjustment, 1962
In the Cool of the Day, 1963
Sunday in New York, 1964
Joy House, 1964
Circle of Love, 1964
Cat Ballou, 1965
The Chase, 1966
Any Wednesday, 1966
The Game Is Over, 1966
Hurry Sundown, 1967
Barefoot in the Park, 1967
Barbarella, 1968
Spirits of the Dead, 1969
They Shoot Horses Don't They?, 1969
Klute, 1971
F.T.A. (Free the Army), 1972
Tout Va Bien, 1972
Steelyard Blues, 1973
A Doll's House, 1973
Introduction to the Enemy, 1974
The Blue Bird, 1976
Fun With Dick and Jane, 1977
Julia, 1977
Coming Home, 1978
Comes a Horseman, 1978
California Suite, 1978
The China Syndrome, 1979
The Electric Horseman, 1979
Nine to Five, 1980
Rollover, 1981
On Golden Pond, 1981

OPPOSITE PAGE

LEFT TOP: Newlyweds Jane Fonda and Robert Redford in *Barefoot in the Park*. The bride accuses the groom of being a stuffed-shirt lawyer who can't let loose. "We share the same causes," Fonda remarked of her long-time friendship with Redford.

LEFT BOTTOM: In *Klute*, Fonda, a call girl who sees a psychiatrist to figure out her motivation for being a prostitute, acts as bait to help Donald Sutherland, a detective, lure a vicious murderer.

RIGHT: Fonda did a nude striptease behind the opening titles of *Barbarella*. The spacey movie of the sci-fantasy comic strip was directed by her first husband, Roger Vadim, whom she denounced a decade later for his "sexual exploitation of women."

LEFT: Robert Redford got top billing and a salary reported to be three times as large as Jane Fonda's in *The Electric Horseman*, in which she played a career-minded TV news reporter to his rebellious cowboy.

ABOVE: Called "Hanoi Jane" for her anti–Vietnam War statements, Fonda used a double for the nude lovemaking scene with Jon Voight in *Coming Home*.

Dustin Hoffman Underdog

Real name: Dustin Hoffman; Born: August 8, 1937
Academy Award; Best Actor, Kramer vs. Kramer

Among the most popular superstars of the 1980s, only E.T. The Extra-Terrestrial is shorter and more of an outsider than 5'6" Dustin Hoffman. In melodramas that have interpreted and shaped cultural values, his sympathetic, defenseless males are always embroiled in love-hate conflicts and situations beyond their control. He was the affluent middle-class dropout in *The Graduate*; the persecuted, pioneering comedian in *Lenny*; the single father of *Kramer vs. Kramer*; and the unemployed actor in *Tootsie*.

Acting opened up the world of women to the skinny nerd who grew up with a big nose, fantasies of being James Dean, and fears of not being sociable or athletic enough. "It's a great way to meet girls. I felt attractive for the first time," he says. More than a means of self-expression, acting is the group therapy part of psychoanalysis for Hoffman, who considers all actors underdogs.

His best roles examine the feminine side of his personality. The actor in *Tootsie* becomes a better man by becoming a woman. "It's shallow to judge people by the way they look," he says. "But if I'd met Dorothy Michaels at a party, I'd have passed on her physically as a write-off. In a sense, I was rejecting myself. I was a male Dorothy. Women passed me over for the same reason." Of *Kramer vs. Kramer*, the film that mirrored his own experiences as a divorced father, Hoffman contends, "I was a bad father who tried to be a good mother." Meryl Streep, his co-star in the movie, believes that what Dustin Hoffman would really like to do is to give birth. "I feel cheated," he moans, "never being able to know what it's like to get pregnant, carry a child, and breast feed."

LEFT: Dustin Hoffman's Benjamin Braddock is seduced by Anne Bancroft's Mrs. Robinson in *The Graduate*.

BELOW: In *Tootsie*, Hoffman masquerades as Dorothy Michaels, who becomes the star of a TV soap opera.

ABOVE: In *Kramer vs. Kramer*, Justin Henry with his movie father, Dustin Hoffman, whose wife leaves him to find herself.

LEFT: Hoffman, Meryl Streep, and Henry in *Kramer vs. Kramer*. The film reflected the effects of women's liberation on the American family and the trauma of divorce on parents and children.

OPPOSITE: Dustin Hoffman and Andy Warhol from *Tootsie*. The idea for the role-reversal comedy germinated when screenwriter Murray Schisgal asked Hoffman, "What kind of a woman would you be if you were a woman? How would your life be different?" The actor's regret was that his Dorothy Michaels would never be pretty, though in the movie he/she becomes a media darling, appearing on the covers of *Ms.*, and *Cosmopolitan*.

LEFT: In *The Graduate*, Dustin Hoffman —depressed, confused, and undecided about his future—has a clandestine affair with Anne Bancroft, who is married to his father's business partner.

ABOVE: Dustin Hoffman as the tubercular and pathetic con man Ratso Rizzo, and Jon Voight as the cowboy stud and male hustler Joe Buck in *Midnight Cowboy*.

OPPOSITE: Hoffman doing one of Lenny Bruce's outrageous nightclub comedy monologues in the film biography *Lenny*. His portrayal of the brilliant, arrogant, and foul-mouthed comedian made Bruce into a nice, mixed-up Jewish boy who was persecuted for his use of obscene material and drugs.

Warren Beatty
Superstud

Real Name: Warren Beaty; Born: March 30, 1937; Academy Award: Best Director, Reds

He tackled comedy and violence in *Bonnie and Clyde.* He settled the score on sex and politics in *Shampoo.* And in the popcorn sports comedy *Heaven Can Wait,* Warren Beatty, Hollywood's only genuine Don Juan, conquered death and the Super Bowl.

In *Shampoo,* his steamy spoof of 1960s sexual manners and mores, Beatty explains what motivates a compulsive superstud and why George, the Casanova hairdresser he plays, can't be satisfied by one woman. In the movie, George is asked why, in the course of one day, he hops in and out of bed with his steady girlfriend (Goldie Hawn), his rival's wife (Lee Grant), his rival's mistress (Julie Christie), and his rival's daughter (Carrie Fisher). As though it were the

most logical of rationales, the superstud meekly replies, "Because it makes me feel that I could live forever."

Money has occupied as much of Beatty's time as movies and women. As his older sister, actress Shirley MacLaine, commented, "Warren's very much into money. When you have made a lot of money people take you seriously." But it's his image as a superstud that fills box-office coffers and gossip columns. The closest Beatty has ever come to confirming or denying his celebrated sexual powers is the statement, "If I tried to keep up with what is said of me sexually, I would be, as Frank Sinatra once said, speaking to you from a jar in the University of Chicago Medical Center."

No matter who his Academy Award–

winning paramour of the moment happens to be, Warren Beatty appears never to be able to love anyone more than he loves himself. Whether women leave him or he drops them, he always moves on to the next woman and film. When asked if he would like to do something more serious than make sex comedies, he responded, "Is there anything more serious than that?"

BELOW AND OPPOSITE: In *Heaven Can Wait,* Warren Beatty, who was captain of his high school football team in Arlington, Virginia, played Joe Pendleton, a Los Angeles Rams quarterback prematurely called to the great football field in the sky. The superstud superstar demands a recall and is supernaturally returned to earth as the head of an international conglomerate.

ABOVE LEFT: Warren Beatty's romance with the late Natalie Wood broke up her marriage to Robert Wagner, whom she later remarried.

ABOVE RIGHT: Expanding his reputation as a heartbreaker, Beatty was named correspondent in a divorce suit brought against Leslie Caron by her husband, Peter Hall.

LEFT: With his Elvis Presley pompadour and his James Dean look of seething vulnerability, Warren Beatty set Natalie Wood's and everyone else's heart on fire in *Splendor in the Grass*, his first movie.

OPPOSITE: As the bank robbers Bonnie Parker and Clyde Barrow, Faye Dunaway and Warren Beatty excited moviegoers in *Bonnie and Clyde*. Beatty's first venture at producing altered the traditional gangster format with its hip humor, Clyde's impotence, the slow-motion death scenes, and the flashy air of nostalgia for America's outlaw past.

ABOVE: Warren Beatty blow-dries Julie Christie's hair in *Shampoo*. Of George, "the cut 'em and lay 'em hairdresser" he plays in the film, Beatty comments, "A hairdresser is the equivalent of a truck driver in Beverly Hills."

LEFT: The *Shampoo* triangle—Julie Christie, Warren Beatty, and Goldie Hawn. Beatty and Christie's six-year relationship, his most serious with any woman, broke up before the filming of *Shampoo*.

RIGHT: Beatty, who contends that "even the promiscuous feel pain," commutes by motorcyle to his *Shampoo* clientele.

In *Reds*, an ambitious but preachy 200-minute history lesson on capitalism versus communism, Beatty cast himself as John Reed, the American journalist and revolutionary who wrote *Ten Days That Shook the World*, and Diane Keaton as Louise Bryant, Reed's wife. Though it is set against the background of the Russian Revolution, the political drama has more to do with the couple's stormy marriage than with socialism. Because of Beatty and Keaton's highly publicized off-camera romance and celebrity singles status, audiences found it difficult to accept them as passionately committed activists.

In Warren We Trust: A Beatty souvenir.

187

Jack Nicholson Odd Man Out

Real name: John Joseph Nicholson; Born: April 22, 1937
Academy Award: Best Actor, One Flew Over the Cuckoo's Nest
Best Supporting Actor, Terms of Endearment

A veteran of grade B horror, teen killer, and motorcycle flicks, Jack Nicholson is the wild man of movies and movie stars. His soul-searching weirdos and sensitive psychos regard their rebellion against authority as virtuous. Appreciated for his absurd sense of humor and wicked smile, the disconcerting odd man out delights in attacking audiences' values because he feels it's good for them.

"I'm at least seventy-five percent of every character I play," he says. Revered for his thoroughness and abandonment as an actor, his specialty is pulling out all the stops in a character's personality to let anger, rage, and emotional truth hang out. Nicholson's "bullshit artist" side slips into his finest performances: the funky lawyer in *Easy Rider*, who's stoned out of his mind on marijuana and who babbles about creatures from outerspace; the private investigator in *Chinatown*, who disdains conventional society and political cover-ups; and the out-of-control mental patient, McMurphy, in *One Flew Over the Cuckoo's Nest*.

Nicholson's greatest pleasures are women and marijuana. "I get high about four days a week. I think that's average for an American," he jokes, refusing to advocate anything for anybody. Because of his role in *Carnal Knowledge* as an inveterate womanizer whose search for the perfect girl leads to frustration and impotence, the actor earned the reputation of being a male chauvinist pig. In his own life, he contends that he tries to be honest with women except "when you're with a chick and you ball somebody else. It's hard to tell the truth in that situation. I've tried it."

BELOW: Jack Nicholson hits the road with dope dealers Dennis Hopper and Peter Fonda in the counter-culture biker film *Easy Rider*.

RIGHT: In *One Flew Over the Cuckoo's Nest*, Nicholson was McMurphy, the psycho-rebel of a mental hospital ward.

The Cry Baby Killer, 1958
Too Soon to Love, 1960
Studs Lonigan, 1960
The Wild Ride, 1960
The Little Shop of Horrors, 1961
The Broken Land,1962
The Raven, 1963
The Terror, 1963
Ensign Pulver, 1964
Back Door to Hell, 1964
Flight to Fury, 1964
Ride in the Whirlwind, 1965
The Shooting, 1965
The St. Valentine's Day Massacre, 1967
Hell's Angels on Wheels, 1967
Rebel Rousers, 1967
Psych-Out, 1968
Easy Rider, 1969
On a Clear Day You Can See Forever, 1970
Five Easy Pieces, 1970
Drive, He Said, 1971
Carnal Knowledge, 1971
A Safe Place, 1971
The King of Marvin Gardens, 1972
The Last Detail, 1973
Chinatown, 1974
Tommy, 1975
The Passenger, 1975
The Fortune, 1975
One Flew Over the Cuckoo's Nest, 1975
The Missouri Breaks, 1976
The Last Tycoon, 1976
Goin' South, 1978
The Shining, 1980
The Postman Always Rings Twice, 1981
Reds, 1981
The Border, 1982
Terms of Endearment, 1983

Broadcasting his killer smile and vampire teeth, a homicidal Jack Nicholson screams ''Heeeeere's Johnny,'' in the movie of Stephen King's novel The Shining.

LEFT AND BELOW: As *Chinatown*'s cynical private eye with a proclivity for jumping to premature conclusions, Nicholson falls in love with Faye Dunaway, a mysterious widow who hires him to investigate the death of her husband.

OPPOSITE: Nicholson plays basketball with inmates William Duell and Will Sampson in *One Flew Over the Cuckoo's Nest.*

LEFT: Nicholson with soul mate and fellow girl watcher Warren Beatty.

BELOW: In front of his art collection, Nicholson toys with a plate of shredded money. "It creates more interest than any other art in the room," he says.

Faye Dunaway
Liberated Lady

Real name: Dorothy Faye Dunaway; Born: January 14, 1941; Academy Award: Best Actress, Network

When Boswell said to Dr. Johnson, "Men know that women are an over-match for them," he might have had Faye Dunaway in mind. Sensational at conveying the turbulence, demonic passion, and determination of iron-willed women, the green-eyed blonde specializes in playing heroines crazed by their desire to get what they want. "I've never known an actress to take work as seriously as she does. I tell you she is a maniac," said *Chinatown* co-star Jack Nicholson, who himself has been singled out for the attention to detail that he brings to his work.

In *Bonnie and Clyde*, *Network*, and *Mommie Dearest*, Dunaway constructs women with merit, infallible instincts, intelligence, and experience equal to that of a man—plus the skill of knowing how to beat men at their own game. For the part of Bonnie Parker, Dunaway shed thirty pounds, making the bank robber lean, tough, and mean. "The biggest thing about Bonnie was her frustration," says Dunaway. "She was up against a stone wall—a girl with potential who is blocked." In *Network*, the liberated lady proved she could be a bigger corporate monster and power broker than her male colleagues.

The other characteristic of a Dunaway woman is that she demands equal power in any male-female relationship. Once she and a man are mutually attracted, she insists on a fifty-fifty say in the ensuing attachment. If it isn't there, she leaves or retaliates, just the way a man would. After her romance with Italian actor Marcello Mastroianni, Dunaway realized "to make your lover happy and at ease when you're dying inside is to kill a relationship."

Like other movie actresses, she complains about the scarcity of positive action roles for women in stage, screen, and television. She's irked because women have changed and "writers can't keep up with us." Put down and praised for being self-sufficient, insecure, disciplined, and prone to crying, Faye Dunaway maintains that just because she has always portrayed calculating, tense, driven women doesn't mean she is one of them.

BELOW: Dunaway as the "castrating bitch" and power-hungry television executive in *Network*, one of the most important roles written for a woman in the 1970s.

OPPOSITE: In the 1930s gothic-style thriller *Chinatown*, Dunaway was the mysterious Evelyn Mulwray, who's trying to hide the fact that she'd been raped by her father and given birth to their child.

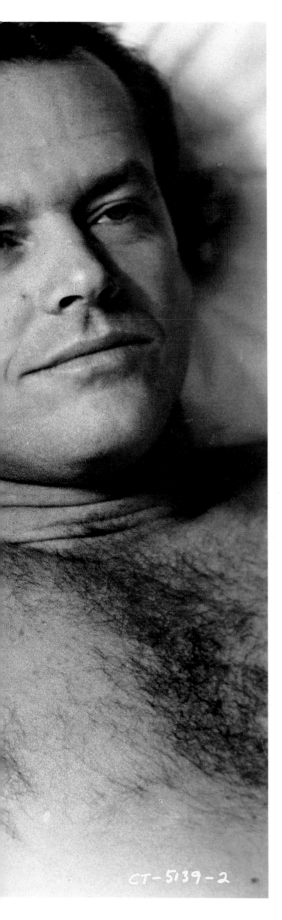

CT-5139-2

MD-44-17

LEFT: Faye Dunaway and Jack Nicholson in a love scene from *Chinatown*. "About acting," says Nicholson, "Faye is usually right."

TOP: In the campy horror movie *Mommie Dearest*, Dunaway went berserk as the alcoholic and egomaniacal movie star

Joan Crawford, who beats her adopted daughter, Christina, with a wire coat hanger.

BOTTOM LEFT: Faye Dunaway kept the birth of her son, Liam, by photographer Terry O'Neill a secret from the press.

BOTTOM RIGHT: O'Neill and Dunaway.

LEFT: When *Bonnie and Clyde* producer Warren Beatty first saw Faye Dunaway, he mistook her for Brigitte Bardot. After the movie's success, she became an imitated "fashion moll."

ABOVE: As the television programming executive in *Network*, Dunaway lives "for a thirty share and a twenty rating." In the course of Paddy Chayefsky's screenplay, the shrewd and competitive businesswoman turns the evening news into a variety show.

The Happening, 1967
Hurry Sundown, 1967
Bonnie and Clyde, 1967
The Thomas Crown Affair, 1968
The Extraordinary Seaman, 1969
A Place for Lovers, 1969
The Arrangement, 1969

Little Big Man, 1970
Puzzle of a Downfall Child, 1971
Doc, 1971
The Deadly Trap, 1972
Oklahoma Crude, 1973
The Three Musketeers, 1974
Chinatown, 1974
The Towering Inferno, 1974

The Four Musketeers, 1975
Three Days of the Condor, 1975
Network, 1976
Voyage of the Damned, 1977
Eyes of Laura Mars, 1978
The Champ, 1979
The First Deadly Sin, 1980
Mommie Dearest, 1981
The Wicked Lady, 1983

Al Pacino
Godfather

Real name: Alfred Pacino; Born: April 25, 1940

Insisting on his own moral and esthetic code, Al Pacino proved he was Marlon Brando's artistic descendant by vaulting into overnight fame in *The Godfather.* ("We are all indebted to Brando," says Pacino.) His chiaroscuro film portait of Michael Corleone, the vengeful Mafia businessman who eliminates his family's rivals, outclasses all the other misfits and loners in his movie gallery. Pacino's hippie cop informer in *Serpico* and his incompetent homosexual bank robber in *Dog Day Afternoon* never captured the public's imagination to the same extent as the ruthless Mafia scion.

At first Michael Corleone refuses to participate in the family's activities. He becomes a killer out of loyalty when he avenges the attempt on his father's life. But power rots him and he becomes estranged from his wife and family. At the finish of *The Godfather,*

Part II, he is a despiritualized, expressionless man. Like Michael Corleone, the complicated Al Pacino has difficulty sustaining personal relationships, especially with women. In his own life he admits, "I have not gone into or resolved many things."

The high school dropout, who has won many awards for his stage acting, was born an only child in the Bronx. His parents divorced when he was two, and he was raised by his grandparents (one of his grandfathers came from Corleone, Sicily). Like Brando, Pacino has a certain contempt for movie acting. His first love is the stage. In the midst of *The Godfather* glory, he appeared in *The Basic Training of Pavlo Hummel* before audiences of eighty-five people at a small theater.

Moving back and forth from film to theater, the actor has not re-created the impact of his Godfather role, causing

some to wonder if he has lost movie momentum. Critics assert that Pacino, like many of the leading actors of the 1970s and 1980s, would have been a character actor in movies of the 1930s and 1940s. The power of his image will be tested in the remake of *Scarface*, in which Pacino plays a Cuban refugee who becomes an underworld drug czar until his downfall.

BELOW: In *Dog Day Afternoon*, based on a true story, Pacino was the hysterical Sonny, who robs a bank to pay for his boyfriend's sex-change operation.

OPPOSITE: Pacino as Michael Corleone, the Ivy League—educated organized crime mogul. Though he doesn't become the U.S. Senator his father wanted him to be, he tells the Nevada Senator he buys in *The Godfather, Part II*, "We're all part of the same hypocrisy."

Me, Natalie, 1969
The Panic in Needle Park, 1971
The Godfather, 1972
Scarecrow, 1973
Serpico, 1973
The Godfather, Part II, 1974
Dog Day Afternoon, 1975
Bobby Deerfield, 1977
And Justice for All, 1979
Cruising, 1980
Author! Author!, 1982
Scarface, 1983

As a New York City undercover policeman in *Serpico*, Pacino informed on corrupt colleagues.

ABOVE LEFT: In *The Godfather, Part II*, Michael Corleone orders the execution of his weak, bungling brother Fredo (John Cazale), who inadvertently set up the don for a hit in his home.

ABOVE RIGHT: Jill Clayburgh and Al Pacino lived together for five years. "I have an intense fear of being left," he said. Clayburgh commented, "I found out who my friends were when I broke up with Al. We were all wrong for each other."

RIGHT: In *The Godfather, Part II*, Pacino with Diane Keaton, who played his wife. When she tells him that her miscarriage was really an abortion, "just like our marriage is an abortion," and that she is leaving him, he refuses to let her go. The wives of Godfathers don't walk out on them, but Keaton does.

The Godfather Saga
A Family Affair

The Godfather

Academy Awards: Best Picture; Best Screenplay based on material from another medium, Francis Ford Coppola and Mario Puzo

The Godfather, Part II

Academy Awards: Best Picture; Best Director, Francis Ford Coppola Best Screenplay Adapted from Other Material, Francis Ford Coppola and Mario Puzo

Praised for combining commerce and art, director Francis Ford Coppola's blockbuster epics *The Godfather* and *The Godfather, Part II* marked the spiritual death of the American dream and the American family. The Renaissance moviemaker used organized crime as a metaphor to comment on the corruption of big business. He also became the "godfather of the New Hollywood" by reviving the sequel format that spawned the *Jaws, Superman, Star Wars*, and *Raiders of the Lost Ark* series.

In grand opera style, Coppola fashioned a new gangster movie genre by blending the Mafia code of vendetta with the tradition of loyalty in the Italian-American family. (The Corleones were similar to the Medicis about whom revenge dramas were written.) The director interspersed gang wars with the religious rites of a wedding, funeral, baptism, and first communion. The historiographic notion that "if history has taught us anything—it's that you can kill anyone" was underscored by the pensive Godfather (God-the-father) waltz music and the gorgeous shadowy photography in the films.

The melodrama about the Sicilian orphan who comes to the new country for bread and work and grows rich outside the law in collusion with other immigrants—Jews, Irish, Poles—was part of Coppola's larger statement about greed and abuses of power in business and politics. Criticized for glorifying the Mafia in *The Godfather*, he deliberately set out in *The Godfather, Part II* to destroy the Corleone family and to punish Michael Corleone, who divides the family that Don Vito Corleone held sacred.

In his greatest cinematic achievement, the imaginative U.C.L.A.-trained director had it both ways—allowing audiences to revel in the family's triumphs while condemning the Corleones morally.

BELOW: In *The Godfather*, Don Vito Corleone (Marlon Brando) is gunned down because he refuses to traffic in narcotics with other crime families.

OPPOSITE: Al Pacino, the new don, and Marlon Brando, the old don, in *The Godfather*. Of the succession, Coppola says, "The father presided over the family on its rise, the son on its ruin."

OVERLEAF: The wedding scene that opens *The Godfather*. The adults from left to right: Robert Duvall, Tere Livrano, John Cazale, Gianni Russo, Talia Shire, Morgana King, Marlon Brando, James Caan, and Julia Gregg.

In a flashback from *The Godfather, Part II*, Robert De Niro, as the young Vito Corleone, with his wife (Francesca de Sapio) and children. De Niro and Marlon Brando were the first actors to win Oscars for playing the same character.

The Individualists

Diane Keaton
Annie Hall

Real Name: Diane Hall; Born: January 5, 1946; Academy Award: Best Actress, Annie Hall

No actress-comedienne of the 1970s represented the confused single woman who cannot live up to her personal vision of liberation better than Diane Keaton. Her appeal as the fluffy birdbrain in Woody Allen's *Annie Hall, Play It Again, Sam,* and *Love and Death* lies in her beguiling concoction of weakness and strength. Unlike Katharine Hepburn, the free-thinking movie actress she tries to emulate, the self-doubting Keaton has difficulty making choices and becomes incapable of functioning.

"Diane would get up in the morning and apologize for it," says *Annie Hall* co-star Tony Roberts. Comments Woody Allen, "She feels that what she is doing is not good enough because her standards are so high." According to Keaton's most famous boyfriend, Warren Beatty, who directed and starred with her in *Reds,* "She has a great sense of the terror that a woman can feel who has an insecure identity. And she has a great sense of the comedic aspect of that terror." To these analyses, the basically independent Diane Keaton might reply in her throwaway *Annie Hall* style, "La di da. Well, la di da," her abbreviation for "Hello. Goodbye. This is never going to work out."

The home movie of the mistakes in their relationship, *Annie Hall* was Woody Allen's valentine to Keaton's dithery comic style. Their offbeat romance became as fashionable as her unisex *Annie Hall* look of floppy hats, baggy pants, and men's shirts, ties, and vests. Like her wacky movie alter ego, Keaton loves mayonnaise, uses black soap, has a Grammy Hall, and is afraid of live lobsters.

Keaton's film caricatures of herself as a rejected and trapped woman have been praised for their introspection and derided for their repetition. Many wonder if she will alter the low opinion she holds of her talent, looks, and education; learn to trust herself; and overcome her fear of commitment. "Sometimes," she says, "I think it might be worth forming a strong bond with one person."

BELOW: Keaton admits she's "a nervous wreck around men." When she finds herself attracted to Woody Allen in *Annie Hall,* all she can say is "Oh, oh . . . God. Well. . . . Oh, well, la di da."

OPPOSITE: Keaton in the elegant ragamuffin and expensive cheap-chic *Annie Hall* layered look.

TOP: With Al Pacino in *The Godfather.*

CENTER: In *Looking for Mr. Goodbar,* Keaton, a school teacher, picks up men in bars and is murdered by one of them.

BOTTOM: In *Reds,* Keaton's Louise Bryant was a literary groupie with aspirations married to Warren Beatty's radical journalist John Reed.

An *Annie Hall*-ish portrait of Diane Keaton, who exhibited and published *Reservations*, her photographs of hotel lobbies and interiors.

Woody Allen
Urban Neurotic

Real name: Allen Stewart Konigsberg; Born: December 1, 1935
Academy Awards: Best Director, Annie Hall; Best Original Screenplay, Annie Hall

Life is a concentration camp and deathwatch, and the world is split into "the horrible and the just miserable" for cuddly comic loser Woody Allen. To his joke, "Not only is God dead, but try getting a plumber on weekends," there's the anti-joke, "God died and Woody Allen will never forgive him for it." While many double over with laughter at his self-loathing, others are repelled by the "total heavy-osity" of his personal satire.

Crediting comedians Bob Hope and Mort Sahl as influences, the pessimistic Allen uses his nervous breakdown movies to share with audiences his anhedonia (the inability to experience pleasure), paranoia, problems with women, morbid preoccupation with death, and decades of psychotherapy. There's always a moral to his funny but serious humor in *Play It Again, Sam, Sleeper, Love and Death,* and *Annie Hall,* in which he superbly mixes and matches jokes and sight gags.

In *Everything You Always Wanted to Know About Sex but Were Afraid to Ask,* Allen was hilarious as a frightened sperm reluctant to leave his host. In *Annie Hall,* based on their failed real-life romance, Allen and Diane Keaton overanalyzed their relationship to an early grave. His serious films (*Interiors* and *Stardust Memories*), influenced by Swedish director Ingmar Bergman, don't fare as well with audiences because of the pretension and blocked psyches of his characters.

"Love eases tension. Sex causes tension," pronounced the dissatisfied writer, director, and star of *A Midsummer Night's Sex Comedy.* "I try to have sex only with women I like a lot. Otherwise, I find it fairly mechanical," explains Allen, who phones in for psychotherapy when he's out of town.

OPPOSITE: Joke writer, literary humorist, stand-up comic, and miserable nebbish Woody Allen.

BELOW: Backed by a poster of his mentor Humphrey Bogart, Allen in bed with Diane Keaton, the wife of his best friend in *Play It Again, Sam.*

ABOVE: Wearing an air-filled suit, Allen takes off as the balloonatic in *Sleeper*, his parody of a robotized society.

RIGHT: Urban Jewish neurotic meets suburban Protestant neurotic. In this scene from *Annie Hall*, subtitles were used to convey Allen's true feelings about Keaton. When he tells her, "Photography is a new art form and a set of esthetics has not emerged yet," he's really thinking, "I wonder what she looks like naked."

The comic strip "Inside Woody Allen" was based on the comic loser's problems: life is unfair, his parents don't understand him, he doesn't understand himself, women reject him, and he's constantly getting into situations that he complains about to his psychiatrist.

Woody Allen and Diane Keaton amid the statuary in the Museum of Modern Art's sculpture garden in *Manhattan*. In his docu-comedy slice of contemporary New York life, balance and commitment are complicated and almost impossible to maintain because friends and lovers are "always looking for things to be perfect and unwilling to settle for less."

Jill Clayburgh
Unmarried Woman

Real name: Jill Clayburgh; Born: April 30, 1944

Pretty, putty-faced, down-to-earth Jill Clayburgh is emblematic of the gutsy, single working woman of the 1980s. With dignity and sincerity she tries to cope with a society turned inside out by the shifting sex roles of the last decade. After her husband of sixteen years leaves her, Erica, the heroine of *An Unmarried Woman*, restructures her life through therapy, work, and not letting herself be trapped by love. Of Marilyn, the school teacher in *Starting Over* who's wooed by a divorced Burt Reynolds, Clayburgh says, "People love her because she's everyone looking for love."

Her feminine, intelligent, and competent women included the first woman justice on the Supreme Court in *First Monday in October*, the brainy math teacher of *It's My Turn*, and the valium-addicted television documentary filmmaker with an alcoholic live-in boyfriend in *I'm Dancing as Fast as I Can.*

"I'm a worrier like everyone else," concedes Clayburgh. Her definition of happiness is success through work, which for her constitutes identity. Like her hero Woody Allen, she has been in analysis for a thousand years. "Don't ask me why, but for some reason I was terribly unhappy while growing up. I started to see a shrink in second grade. I was very violent and self-destructive. I began to take analysis seriously at twenty-six and it has helped me more than anything else. I'd be dead without it." When she gets depressed, Clayburgh cooks or jogs.

Because of her unthreatening image, Clayburgh thinks women sympathize with the way her movie heroines deal with the conflicts and pressures of home and career. "They tell me I have the same vices and virtues that they do," she reports. "And, without being jealous, they confide that their husbands want to run off with me."

BELOW: In *An Unmarried Woman*, Clayburgh jogs through Manhattan's upper East Side with Michael Murphy, the husband who leaves her for a younger woman.

OPPOSITE: Jill Clayburgh, the epitome of the divorced, single woman of the 1970s, in *An Unmarried Woman.*

ABOVE LEFT: In *Semi-Tough*, Clayburgh and Burt Reynolds were veterans of "the sexual revolution wars." Reynolds tells her, "You're real close, honey, but you ain't no ten," and runs off with her on the day she's supposed to marry his roommate.

ABOVE RIGHT: Jill Clayburgh, who had her first child at thirty-seven, and husband, playwright David Rabe.

LEFT: "I'm no one-nighter," Clayburgh, a nursery school teacher, informs recently divorced Burt Reynolds in *Starting Over*.

OPPOSITE: "I live on grapes and lettuce, I'm so afraid of putting on weight," said the firm-bodied Clayburgh, who danced in her underpants in *An Unmarried Woman*.

The Wedding Party, 1969
The Telephone Book, 1971
Portnoy's Complaint, 1972
The Thief Who Came to Dinner, 1973
The Terminal Man, 1974
Gable and Lombard, 1976
Silver Streak, 1976
Semi-Tough, 1977
An Unmarried Woman, 1978
Luna, 1979
Starting Over, 1979
It's My Turn, 1980
First Monday in October, 1981
I'm Dancing as Fast as I Can, 1982
Hannah K., 1983

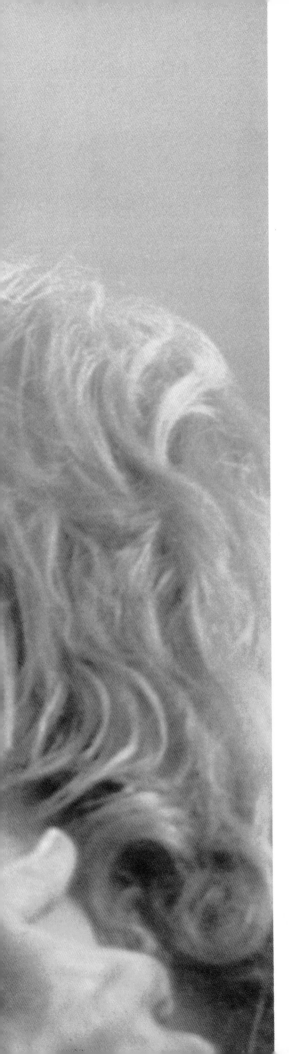

Burt Reynolds
Playboy

Real name: Burton Leon Reynolds, Jr.; Born: February 11, 1936

Burt Reynolds's appeal as the accessible movie star playboy whose greatest desire is to be loved was nourished on television talk shows and in *Cosmopolitan* magazine's first nude centerfold. "I became a star not because of my image, but in spite of it," he says. "I was the only actor ever to go on talk shows to hype a movie and say, 'It's a turkey.'" Mocking his machismo, Reynolds showed what a glib, brash, quick-witted good old boy he was. As for the *Cosmopolitan* centerfold photograph he owns rights to, Reynolds said he posed for it to satirize *Playboy*.

Reynolds compares his show-off action and comedy "Sun Belt classics," *Gator* and *Smokey and the Bandit*, to Chinese food. "Not great pictures, but great entertainment. You might want to go back for more a couple of hours later," he kids. Though *Deliverance* and *The Longest Yard* demonstrated he could stretch beyond two-dimensional, skirt-chasing Charlie Charm characters, he received acclaim for his comic flair in *Semi-Tough*, a spoof of athletes, and *Starting Over*, the flip side of *An Unmarried Woman*.

While everyone is convinced that Burt Reynolds has done a lot to improve male-female communications and that he wants to be loved, no one is sure of his ability to love back over the long term. "When I'm ready to," he says, "I'll get married."

His May–December affair with Dinah Shore ended after five years. And his romance with Sally Field fizzled because when one was ready to get married, the other got cold feet.

LEFT: Reynolds with Goldie Hawn in *Best Friends*, a comedy about a couple who ruin a friendship by getting married.

BELOW: As Sheriff Earl Ed Dodd, Reynolds in *The Best Little Whorehouse in Texas*.

ABOVE LEFT: In *Hooper*, Reynolds as the world's greatest stuntman.

ABOVE RIGHT: Burt Reynolds proved he could act in *Deliverance*, an essay on man's rape of nature.

LEFT: A football player turned playboy in *The Longest Yard*, Reynolds was forced to participate in a bone-crunching game between prison inmates and guards.

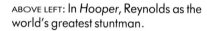

Angel Baby, 1961
Armored Command, 1961
Operation CIA, 1965
Navajo Joe, 1967
Fade-In, 1968
Sam Whiskey, 1969
100 Rifles, 1969
Impasse, 1969
Skullduggery, 1970
Shark!, 1970
Fuzz, 1972
Deliverance, 1972
Everything You Always Wanted to
    Know About Sex but Were Afraid to
    Ask, 1972
Shamus, 1973
The Man Who Loved Cat Dancing,
    1973
White Lightning, 1973
The Longest Yard, 1974
At Long Last Love, 1975

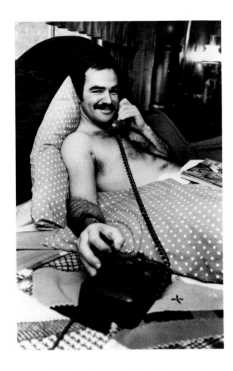

ABOVE: "The only way to handle a reputation for being a sex symbol is to have fun with it. Sex symbols don't last long," says the *Cosmo* centerfold.

ABOVE RIGHT: "If I have any class at all, it's due to Dinah," the playboy complemented the singer-talk show host.

RIGHT: *Smokey and the Bandit* sweethearts Reynolds and Sally Field.

W.W. and the Dixie Dance Kings, 1975
Hustle, 1975
Lucky Lady, 1975
Silent Movie, 1976
Gator, 1976
Nickelodeon, 1976
Smokey and the Bandit, 1977
Semi-Tough, 1977
The End, 1978
Hooper, 1978
Starting Over, 1979
Rough Cut, 1980
Smokey and the Bandit II, 1980
The Cannonball Run, 1981
Paternity, 1981
Sharky's Machine, 1981
The Best Little Whorehouse in Texas, 1982
Best Friends, 1982
Stroker Ace, 1983
The Man Who Loved Women, 1983

Meryl Streep
Madonna

Real name: Mary Louise Streep; Born: June 22, 1949
Academy Awards: Best Supporting Actress, Kramer vs. Kramer; Best Actress: Sophie's Choice

The lustrous and majestically beautiful Meryl Streep has been exalted as the greatest film actress of the 1980s for her suffering Madonna roles. The film star's métier is the problem movie with a sociological message, in which she comes to grips with inner conflicts and disgorges several tangled emotions at the same time. In *The Deer Hunter*, *Kramer vs. Kramer*, and *The French Lieutenant's Woman*, Streep's distraught, ambivalent heroines are composed of equal parts victim and siren.

In superlative performances that are as penetrating as movie acting gets, the Yale Drama School graduate strives to make films more like theater. However, some critics and moviegoers complain that they are deprived of the total pleasure of Streep's breathtaking work because of her elegant nervousness and self-conscious mannerisms, elaborated through hand gestures, facial grimaces, and twitchy head movements.

In *Sophie's Choice*, the actress's pathologically intense interpretation of a haunted Polish concentration camp survivor drew raves as she moved back and forth from Sophie Zawistowska's harrowing past to her doomed future. Streep learned German and Polish for the film's half-hour flashback to the Nazi death camp Auschwitz. She was masterful in conveying the powerlessness of a mother who struggles desperately but in vain to save her children and who lives with the guilt of having outlived loved ones.

The cool and controlled Streep, who may be too intelligent to be a movie star, acknowledges that "the greatest actors and actresses are not necessarily the greatest movie stars and vice versa." But among her peers, she has no competitors as an actress. As for star quality, the wistful beauty with the sorrowful Madonna countenance resembles the great Renaissance paintings *Portrait of Battista Sforza* by Piero della Francesca and *Lady in Yellow* by Alesso Baldovinetti.

Concerned about sexism in film and new methods of male contraception, "the Eleanor Roosevelt of actresses" has undertaken a film about Karen Silkwood, the anti-nuclear activist who was mysteriously killed in an automobile crash.

OPPOSITE: *Kramer vs. Kramer* director Robert Benton allowed Streep to write her own lines for the movie's emotionally intense courtroom custody fight.

BELOW: Divorced parents Dustin Hoffman and Meryl Streep argue about their son in *Kramer vs. Kramer*.

LEFT: In *The Deer Hunter*, Streep becomes involved with Robert De Niro, recently returned from the Vietnam War. Some viewers felt the actress's upper-class Madonna looks and overwrought acting belied her credibility as the supermarket clerk Linda, who waits for a man to "make her life happen."

BELOW: Streep sang and danced in the Off-Broadway musical of *Alice in Wonderland*. "I have a Shavian need for theater to have a message, to pull society up short. It never works of course," says the versatile actress.

ABOVE: Accused of having an affair with a naval officer in *The French Lieutenant's Woman*, Streep was heartbreaking as a melancholy Victorian heroine and victimized governess whose passion and intelligence were ahead of her time.

RIGHT: Meryl Streep with her husband, sculptor Don Gummer, at the Academy Awards ceremonies where she received the Oscar for best supporting actress in *Kramer vs. Kramer*.

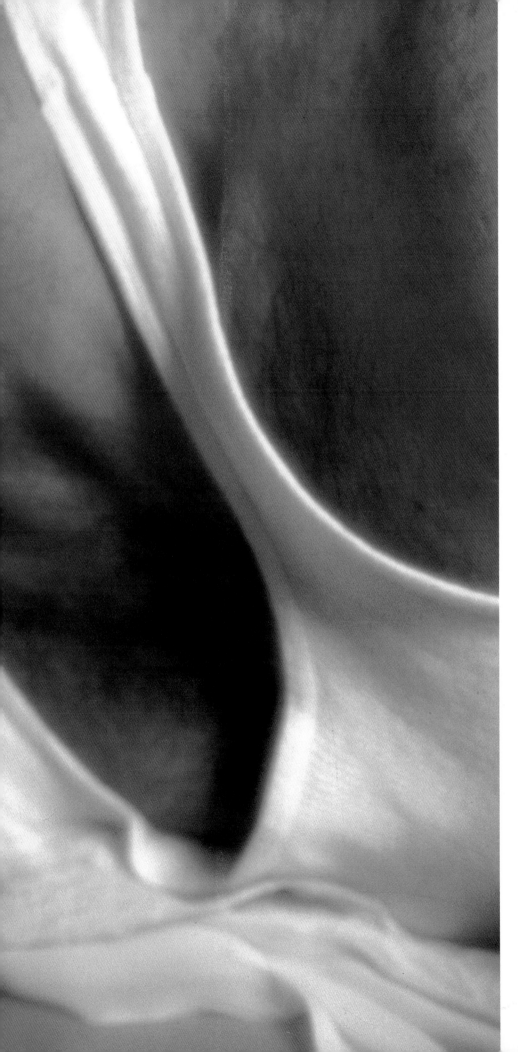

Kevin Kline, Sophie Zawistowska's mad, schizophrenic lover Nathan, and the beatific Meryl Streep in *Sophie's Choice*.

Robert De Niro
Macho Man

Real name: Robert De Niro; Born: August 17, 1943
Academy Awards: Best Supporting Actor, The Godfather, Part II; *Best Actor,* Raging Bull

Non-hero and anti-star Robert De Niro pulverizes audiences with his isolated and uncompromising macho men. Outgrowths of a diseased and fragmented society, his hypnotic sociopaths and fixated voyeurs don't want to be part of any system. Their emotional withdrawal and impulsive outbursts of violence serve as perverse pleas for help. De Niro's sexually guilty and misogynistic 1950s throwbacks seek domination over women, regarding them as temptresses and sex as a depletion of masculinity.

The rage of De Niro's unredemptive characters is that of men who want to be someone else. Very often they don't know who that person is. *Mean Streets'* irresponsible creep Johnny Boy, *Taxi Driver's* hypertense outcast Travis Bickle, and *Raging Bull's* volcanic boxer Jake LaMotta vented their fury by blowing up mailboxes, attacking pimps, or beating up wives and battering opponents in the ring.

The fanatical De Niro incessantly researches his compulsive and insinuating loners. For Vito Corleone in *The Godfather, Part II*, the actor went to Sicily to study a specific dialect and soak up the atmosphere; for *Taxi Driver* he got a hack license and drove a cab; and in *Raging Bull*, he trained with former middleweight champion LaMotta and gained fifty pounds to depict the boxer in his decline as a comic in sleazy clubs. Says De Niro, "It takes a certain kind of person to be a fighter, a certain kind of anger, maybe caused by parents."

A product of Little Italy's spaghetti jungle, the New York City macho man's first performance, at age ten, was as the cowardly lion in a school production of *The Wizard of Oz*. Acting is a matter of life and death for De Niro and he rummages through his characters' psyches until he uncovers what he believes is the clinical truth about their existence. "His life is spent preparing for the next role," says a friend.

As extreme, prideful, and unapproachable as his movie counterparts, Robert De Niro hates to give interviews because he feels they dissipate his acting energy, even though he can be long-winded on acting as art shoptalk. "Technique is concrete," he maintains. "I want to do things that will last because they have substance and quality, not some affectation or style."

OPPOSITE: In *The Deer Hunter*, a taciturn De Niro escaped from a Viet Cong prison camp by playing Russian roulette.

BELOW: As Travis Bickle in *Taxi Driver*, De Niro was a time bomb who exploded by killing the pimp of twelve-year-old prostitute Jodie Foster. John Hinckley's interpretation of the film resulted in his love for Foster and attempted assassination of President Ronald Reagan.

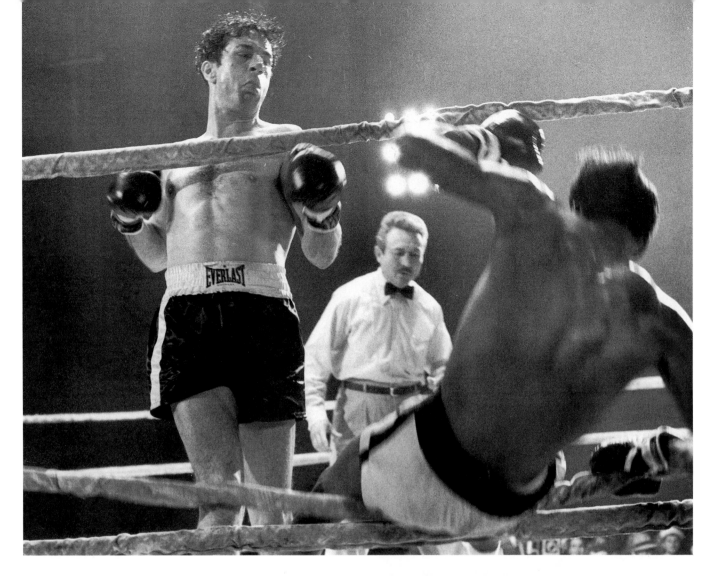

OPPOSITE PAGE

TOP AND BOTTOM: In *The Godfather, Part II*, the Americanized crime boss Vito Corleone returns to Sicily to avenge the murders of his mother and father. Using the same rasping voice that Marlon Brando invented for the don in *The Godfather*, De Niro was considered "compensation for Brando's absence in the sequel."

ABOVE AND RIGHT: Director Martin Scorsese termed *Raging Bull*— one of his *nouveau film noir* exercises in macho obsession—a docu-drama of Jake (The Bronx Bull) LaMotta's life and career. For the part of the boxing champion, De Niro surged from 160 to 212 pounds to authenticate the out-of-condition LaMotta in his nightclub show. Detractors regarded this device as a gimmick unworthy of the nobility of De Niro's astonishing powers of illusion. Admirers considered it the pinnacle of Method acting.

Brooke Shields
Pretty Baby

Real name: Brooke Christa Shields; Born May 31, 1965

Sultry, twelve-year-old Brooke Shields became Hollywood's youngest sex symbol in the erotic soft-core art film *Pretty Baby*. "It's only a role. I'm not going to grow up and be a prostitute," said the "kiddie porn star," who started her career as an Ivory Snow baby and was posing nude for photographers by age nine. Polite, seemingly unspoiled, and very hardworking, Shields comes across as phenomenally bland in films with scripts that reviewers pan for being as coy and unbearable as her dramatic abilities.

The beautiful teenager with the face of a twenty-five-year-old may be a threat to women, but men are attracted by her image as a child-woman seductress who offers favors without expecting anything in return. Managed by her mother, Teri Shields, the star propagated her "Alice in Hookerland" image in *Blue Lagoon* and *Endless Love*. These dreary teenage-lust-and-love flicks were fleshed out with nude and semi-nude scenes by Shields or her double.

The consummate symbol of Hollywood's corruption of innocence, the 5'11" tall, flat-chested Shields has used her androgynous sex appeal to sell jeans in television commercials and to market her lethargic films. In *Sahara*, based on the 1921 silent Valentino classic *The Sheik*, she disguises herself as a boy to enter a desert sports car race and is abducted by a sheik. In private, Shields is swamped with diamonds and gifts from Arab princes, and a royal Grace Kelly-style wedding is not unlikely.

But, as a producer noted, "Brooke's one constant love will always be her mother." The twosome have been inseparable since Teri Shields's divorce from Brooke's father soon after her baby's birth. The mother and daughter are noted for exchanging quips and kisses on movie sets and at restaurants. "This is a superstar, a legend, an Oscar winner," the mother brags of the daughter, whose pretty-baby career she has parlayed into the multi-million-dollar Brooke Shields and Company, Inc. To charges that she's been exploited by her mother, Brooke Shields responds, "If I wanted to stop, she'd let me."

BELOW: In the teen sexcapade *Blue Lagoon*, Shields found an ideal mate in Christopher Atkins, whose good looks and lack of acting ability matched her own. Shipwrecked on a desert island, the nubile pair discover sex and subsequently have a baby.

OPPOSITE: In *Pretty Baby*, Shields, as the daughter of a whore, grows up in a New Orleans brothel and marries photographer E. J. Bellocq, whose photographs of prostitutes inspired the film.

LEFT: Susan Sarandon was Brooke Shields's prostitute mother in *Pretty Baby*.

BELOW: As the angelic hooker who's auctioned off in *Pretty Baby*, Shields whispered to her buyer, "I can feel the steam coming right through my dress."

The tantalizing and enticing child model
with sea-blue eyes, vanilla complexion,
chestnut mane, and provocative pout.

ABOVE: Christopher Atkins and Shields in their *Blue Lagoon* designer loincloths.

LEFT: Pretty baby Brooke and mother-agent Teri Shields. The mother-and-daughter team are in harmony most of the time but have a reputation for fighting and making up at photographer's studios, on movie sets, and at discos. "There's a lot of love and hate in a relationship as close and complicated as theirs is. It would make a fascinating blockbuster movie," says a friend.

OPPOSITE: In the controversial Calvin Klein jeans commercial that increased sales by 300 percent in ninety days and was temporarily banned by some television stations, Shields teased, "You know what comes between me and my Calvins? Nothing."

Calvin Klein Jeans

John Travolta
Pretty Boy

Real Name: John Travolta; Born: February 18, 1954

The greasy Sweathog of prime time's "Welcome Back Kotter" was the first TV idol to cross over to movie stardom. In his white, three-piece kingpin suit, sensual John Travolta bolted onto the screen in *Saturday Night Fever* with a series of electrifying disco dances. After flying into the role of the dancing gang leader in *Grease*, the pretty-faced poster boy and his roller coaster career temporarily bottomed out. He was unconvincing as a beach boy in love with an older woman in the ill-conceived *Moment by Moment* and as the rhinestone cowpoke in the medium hit *Urban Cowboy*.

What his vulnerable, hunky hoods-with-a-heart do best is to start sexual juices flowing. "I have a fortunate thing," explains Travolta about his magnetism. "I don't know whether it's my light eyes or presence, but I have to do very little." To fight off the mobs who grab at him wherever he goes, the cautious star travels with several bodyguards.

Travolta, who left high school in tenth grade to do summer stock and dinner theater, spent his childhood in front of the TV set doing free-form tap dance imitations of his hero Jimmy Cagney in *Yankee Doodle Dandy*. Unconcerned with typecasting, he revived the flashy disco prince Tony Manero as a professional dancer hungry to become a star on Broadway in *Staying Alive*, the *Saturday Night Fever* movie spin-off directed by Sylvester (*Rocky*) Stallone. For their next project, sequel meister Stallone and a newly conditioned John Travolta plan to tackle *Godfather III*.

LEFT: Setting dance and fashion trends, Travolta takes over the floor at Brooklyn's 2001 Odyssey disco in *Saturday Night Fever*.

BELOW: The Travolta charm flopped in the disappointing *Moment by Moment*, in which he had an affair with an older woman played by Lily Tomlin.

OPPOSITE PAGE

TOP: *Grease*, the top-grossing musical in movie history, featured Travolta and Olivia Newton-John in "pre-fab" rock and roll production numbers.

BOTTOM: The Valentino of the 1970s: Travolta as pretty boy Tony Manero in *Saturday Night Fever*.

ABOVE: Travolta mounted on the mechanical bull in *Urban Cowboy*.

RIGHT: A *Saturday Night Fever* sequel, *Staying Alive* takes place six years later with Travolta as a Broadway chorus boy burning to make it on the Great White Way. Cynthia Rhodes is the girlfriend who waits out his infatuation with another dancer.

Sissy Spacek Country Girl

Real name: Mary Elizabeth Spacek; Born: December 25, 1949
Academy Award: Best Actress, Coal Miner's Daughter

Waiflike Sissy Spacek brings an uncanny mutability to her movie roles of real-life women who resolve problems with themselves, loved ones, and the world around them. The characters that the "American primitive" actress has portrayed in true-story films include the nymphet girlfriend of a mass murderer (based on Charles Starkweather) in *Badlands*, the rags-to-riches country music queen Loretta Lynn in *Coal Miner's Daughter*, and the young wife whose husband was killed in a 1970s South American political uprising in *Missing*. At the opposite end of the reality meter, Spacek gave a sensational rendering of the sweet-looking high school monster with supernatural powers in *Carrie*.

"I imitate everyone—thank goodness there's not an elephant around," says the movie star, who's a sprightly combination of down-home charm and ornery gumption. A majorette, cheerleader, and beauty pageant runner-up from Quitman, Texas, Spacek originally set out to be a rock and roll star. She was the official choice of singer Loretta Lynn for the movie of her autobiography, *Coal Miner's Daughter*. Aging from thirteen to thirty-five, Spacek traced Lynn's life from poverty, marriage, and babies to top ten country music fame. The actress was startling in the way she detailed the whiny and goody-goody sides of Loretta Lynn and handled the singer's problems with drugs.

Without making them pious or unpalatable, Sissy Spacek digs out the hope that keeps the facile and uprooted women she plays going. A "hippie Ophelia with clean scrubbed looks," the country girl has set up a company to produce, write, and direct her own films. "I've always wanted to play a sexy chorus girl or a lady wrestler," she says.

BELOW: Freckle-faced Spacek as a teenager sold into white slavery in her movie debut, *Prime Cut*.

OPPOSITE: Spacek "snitched" clothes from Loretta Lynn's wardrobe to wear in the movie of *Coal Miner's Daughter*.

SENIOR PROM

ABOVE: An unpopular high school wall-flower and telekinetic weirdo in *Carrie*, blood-soaked Spacek wreaks havoc on her classmates during prom night.

LEFT: Replacing her Texas twang with a Kentucky drawl, Sissy Spacek did her own singing as country music star Loretta Lynn in *Coal Miner's Daughter*.

OPPOSITE PAGE

TOP: In the political thriller *Missing*, Jack Lemmon and Spacek were Ed and Beth Horman—a real-life father and daughter-in-law searching for her husband, a young American writer who was murdered in a South American coup.

BOTTOM: The rambunctious Sissy Spacek takes a plunge.

Harrison Ford Maverick

Real name: Harrison Ford; Born: July 13, 1942

With his rugged charm, Harrison Ford got the glamour jobs of the century as the space cowboy in *Star Wars* and the renegade archaeologist in *Raiders of the Lost Ark*—movies in which actors played "talking furniture" to state-of-the art special effects. The sci-fantasy and adventure flickeramas he's appeared in have earned more money than those of any performer in film history. "I don't want to be a movie star," says Ford. "I want to be in movies that are stars." His self-effacement is unwarranted because he's the only actor in a Steven Spielberg or George Lucas film who's thrilling enough to steal scenes from special effects.

As the mercenary starpilot Han Solo in *Star Wars*, Ford spoofed Humphrey Bogart, John Wayne, and Clark Gable with the lines, "What good's a reward if you aren't around to use it"; "I've been from one end of this galaxy to the other"; and "I'd prefer a straight fight to this sneaking around." As *Raid-ers of the Lost Ark*'s shady archae-ologist, Indiana Jones, he's hired by the American government to find a buried treasure before the Nazis get to it and, at the same time, make the world safe for democracy. "I'm just making this up as I go," Ford winked at audiences in *Raiders* as he braved a 500-pound rolling boulder, hordes of snakes, and hundreds of black-booted Nazis. As a post-nuke Sam Spade in the catastrophic future film *Blade Runner*, Ford became the twenty-first century's man with a con-science—a slot left vacant by Hum-phrey Bogart.

What Ford's heroes and heels rely on is common sense, ingenuity, and the knowledge that they have the phys-ical and mental strength to defeat their enemies. "I don't take myself too se-riously. I've never been a film buff, and I've never studied or thought about other actors' work. Actually I think I'm best suited to drawing-room comedy," says "the un-star of the unexciting 1980s." He also doesn't consider movie actors creative artists. "Directors and writers are the poets of the system. The job of the actor is to help tell the story," contends the tongue-in-cheek Ford, whose future is littered with cliff-hanging *Star Wars* and *Raiders of the Lost Ark* sequels. Says the maverick, who always has to have the last word, "They're only movies."

BELOW: Prepared to zap intergalactic foes with his laser gun in *Star Wars*, Han Solo, captain of the souped-up pirate ship the Millennium Falcon, and his faithful compan-ion Chewbacca, a 200-year-old Wookiee, who's a cross between a bear, a dog, and a monkey.

OPPOSITE: In *Raiders of the Lost Ark*, dare-devil Indiana Jones pulls a gun and shoots his opponent, an Arab swordsman. "I in-tend to back up nothing I have ever said or done in a movie. Indiana Jones is tough. I am not tough," insists Ford.

The Phenomena

George Lucas
The Wizard of Star Wars

Real name: George Lucas; Born: May 14, 1944

"He puts on film only the things he loves and has few pretensions about making great films or great art. Consequently, he comes closer than most," said Francis Ford Coppola of his colleague George Lucas. The shy, serious, and reclusive Lucas, a graduate of the University of Southern California, wedded technology and imagination in his *Star Wars* series of customized space operas. His comic book myths, which take place "a long time ago in a galaxy far far away," are rooted in movies of the near past (*Flash Gordon* and *Casablanca*) and reflect "a nostalgia for the future."

The success of the wizard of *Star Wars* and *Raiders of the Lost Ark* is the continuing result of not allowing his vision of space as the land of adventure and the destiny of man to be corrupted by outside influences. His nine-part *Star Wars* series is planned through 2004. Says a high school friend of Lucas, "It would give George great pleasure if thirty years from now you did a cross-section

survey of people in space and they said they got involved in space because they saw *Star Wars* as a kid."

Like Walt Disney, who revolutionized film animation, George Lucas is a propagandist and moralist. In the "LucasWorld" trilogy of *Star Wars*, *The Empire Strikes Back*, and *Return of the Jedi*, the director preaches anti-fascism, the renewal of faith in good technology over evil machinery, and the premise that the world can be saved from the stupidity of humans.

The *Star Wars* tycoon, who loves gadgets, special effects, and the machinery of moviemaking, is happiest "imagining" the creatures, equipment, and toys for his movies. "If I wasn't a filmmaker," he says, "I'd probably be a painter or toymaker." At his movie think tank and studio (located in northern California because of his defiance of the Hollywood deal-making establishment), Lucas has been experimenting with computer-made films that require no actors or directors. "I

learned the system and beat it," comments the director, who outwitted movie industry sharks by retaining rights to all the *Star Wars* sequels.

Of all his film creations, George Lucas would most like to be Indiana Jones of the thrill-a-minute *Raiders of the Lost Ark*, the movie he devised the character and story for and had fellow special effects wunderkind Steven Spielberg direct. "Indy can do anything," raves Lucas about the archaeologist-adventurer. "He's a college professor and he's got his Cary Grant side, too."

BELOW: George Lucas with Sir Alec Guinness, *Star Wars'* Ben Obi-Wan Kenobi.

OPPOSITE: See-Threepio C-3PO (Anthony Daniels), a protocol droid with a British accent, and his sidekick, the beeping, whistling, and tooting robot Artoo-Detoo R2-D2 (Kenny Baker), in *Star Wars*.

ABOVE LEFT: Wielding her laser pistol in *Return of the Jedi*, Princess Leia (Carrie Fisher) makes a brave, bright, and pushy Guinevere, who wants to eliminate evil from the universe.

LEFT: For the cantina scene, *Star Wars'* parody of the classic Western saloon located in the city of Mos Eisley on the planet Tatooine, make-up artists created grotesque outerspace varmints.

ABOVE: The light saber (laser sword) duel in *Star Wars* between Ben Obi-Wan Kenobi and Darth Vader (actor David Prowse with the voice of James Earl Jones).

Obi-Wan prophesizes to the dark Lord of The Sith, "You cannot win, Darth. If you strike me down I shall become more powerful than you can imagine."

ABOVE RIGHT: A Rebel X-Wing fires on an Imperial TIE fighter over the Death Star in this mock-up photograph of models and an optical laser beam painting. Director Lucas spliced together dogfight scenes from fifty old war movies to achieve the slam-bang pace he wanted for the space battles in *Star Wars*.

RIGHT: In *The Empire Strikes Back*, Imperial TIE fighters pursue the Millennium Falcon through an asteroid field.

THX 1138, 1971
American Graffiti, 1973
Star Wars, 1977
More American Graffiti, 1979
The Empire Strikes Back, 1980
Raiders of the Lost Ark, 1981
Twice Upon a Time, 1983
Return of the Jedi, 1983
Indiana Jones and the Temple of
    Doom, 1984

OPPOSITE PAGE

TOP: In *The Empire Strikes Back*, giant four-legged Imperial Walkers shoot lasers at Rebel snowspeeders during a battle on the ice planet Hoth.

BOTTOM: In *Star Wars*, Han Solo's Millennium Falcon is drawn into the Death Star, a space fort the size of a small moon that can destroy whole planets with a single blow.

TOP: In *The Empire Strikes Back*, Luke Skywalker is instructed in the ways of the Force by Jedi master Yoda on the swamp planet Dagobah. Skywalker tells Yoda "I don't believe it," when he raises Luke's X-Wing fighter out of a bog. "That's why you fail," replies the sage, who is mechanically operated by Muppeteer Frank Oz.

CENTER: In *Return of the Jedi*, Luke and his lightsaber triumph in a duel with Darth Vader, who turns out to be his and Leia's father.

BOTTOM: Han Solo, Princess Leia, and Chewbacca are captured in the Endor forest by Imperial forces in *Return of the Jedi*.

Steven Spielberg

Real name: Steven Spielberg

Entrepreneur Steven Spielberg's movies are offsprings of the out-of-this-world pop pulp mentality of comic books, best sellers, film classics, and science-fiction TV shows. Movie junk-food to some, his *Jaws, Close Encounters of the Third Kind, Poltergeist, E.T. The Extra-Terrestrial,* and *Twilight Zone* are semi-religious experiences to others. In these pyrotechnic spectacles, he commingles special effects and average people in tales of contact and friendship between humans and benign aliens and in science-fiction stories of horror and the supernatural.

Spielberg considers his idol Walt Disney his parental conscience and television his stepparent. At age twelve, the director, who is deemed capable of making a movie about a Tupperware party suspenseful, filmed the collision of his Lionel train set. "I'm very middle class," says the moviemaker, who grew up in the suburbs in Ohio, New Jersey, and Arizona. "My tastes and emotions are so typical I have a rapport with the average moviegoer in what I like and dislike."

His *E.T. The Extra-Terrestrial* is considered the 1980s version of *The Wizard of Oz* because the adorable space creature with the expandable neck must return home if he is to survive. Says Spielberg, "Elliott Taylor is the closest thing to my experience of growing up in suburbia as a lonely child. But I was also E.T.'s eyes and had to imagine what it would be like to be a

The Extra-Terrestrial

Born: December 18, 1947

creature visiting Earth and what life would be like from his perspective."

Though he seesaws between what's real and what's not, the writer-director usually sides with what isn't. This disposition is expressed in his movies through children and the adults who have kept their childlike innocence. They are the ones granted audiences with outerspace visitors.

Like his buddy George Lucas, Steven Spielberg is applauded and booed for being a master film technician and storyteller with few original ideas other than idealized childhood fantasies. He maintains that his escapist fairy tales juxtapose people and special effects. "A movie works because of the characters, not the special effects. Audiences empathize with people, not with a shark or a spaceship." Spielberg also believes moviegoers would be very disappointed if he didn't make the sequels to *E.T.* and *Raiders of the Lost Ark.*

Steven Spielberg and his megastar E.T., the superintelligent extra-terrestrial who's the Mickey Mouse of the 1980s. Here, the ten-million-year-old scientist from space blesses the director with his healing finger. "We couldn't find a sex for it," says Spielberg. "Girls think it's a girl; boys, a boy." Constructed by special effects sculptor Carlo Rambaldi, the amazing 40-inch-high E.T. models (mechanical, electronic, and walking) have aluminum and steel skeletons and are covered in gray-green polyurethane and rubber.

ABOVE: Spielberg thinks his movie of *Jaws* was more frightening than the book. Called Bruce by the crew, the mechanical killer shark terrorized the residents of the fictional summer resort of Amity Island.

LEFT: In *Close Encounters of the Third Kind*, the destinies of a mother and son (Melinda Dillon and Cary Guffey) are altered after they are buzzed by a spaceship and receive "mental implants."

RIGHT: Drew Barrymore made the home-sick space traveler's heart-light flutter when she kissed him in *E.T. The Extra-Terrestrial*. Before leaving on the spaceship with the geranium she gives him, E.T. tells Drew, who helped him to talk with her Speak and Spell toy, "B. Good."

BELOW: In *E.T. The Extra-Terrestrial*, Elliott Taylor, with E.T. in his bicycle basket, flies above the forest in search of an appropriate site to set up the alien's improvised communication device for making contact with his people.

OPPOSITE: "Big Mama," the nickname of the mother ship of *Close Encounters of the Third Kind*, hovers over Wyoming's Devil's Tower before landing to discharge and pick up earth passengers.

ABOVE: In *Poltergeist*, a modern ghost story set in surburbia and chock full of television-commercial dialogue, Heather O'Rourke is mysteriously drawn by supernatural forces to the television set as her parents, Craig T. Nelson and Jobeth Williams, look on.

RIGHT: "I'll be right here," E.T. promises Elliott Taylor (Henry Thomas) in *E.T. The Extra-Terrestrial*.

Acknowledgements

For their support of and help with STARS! I would like to express my gratitude to Nai Chang, Marya Dalrymple, Robert I. Freedman, J.R. Hirst, Marriott Kohl, Jane Lahr, John Lynch, Allen Mandel, and Andrew Stewart; to Amy Horton, Chris Pullo, and Ricki Rosen for photo acquisitions; and to photographers Bill King and Frederic Ohringer. For his contribution to the Marx Brothers and research on the biographical data and filmographies, special thanks and appreciation to Peter Dolgenos.

A note of thanks to the American Film Institute, Academy of Motion Picture Arts and Sciences, Columbia University Department of Film, Dartmouth College Film Studies Program, Film Society of Lincoln Center, Library of Congress Motion Picture Section, LIFE Picture Service, MacDowell Colony, Museum of Modern Art Film Study Center, Museum of Modern Art Film Stills Archive, Billy Rose Theater Collection/New York Public Library at Lincoln Center, Donnell Library Film Department New York Public Library, New York University Department of Cinema Studies, RKO Studios' Archives, U.C.L.A. Department of Theater Arts, and the University of Southern California Library and Film School.

For their help, cooperation, and consideration, thanks to Columbia Pictures, a division of Columbia Pictures Industries, Inc., Embassy Pictures, Crown International, The Ladd Company, Lucasfilm Ltd., Metro-Goldwyn-Mayer Inc., MGM/UA Entertainment Co., National Telefilm Associates, Inc., Paramount Pictures Corporation, RKO General Pictures, Twentieth Century-Fox Film Corporation, United Artists Corporation, MCA/Universal Pictures, Viacom International, Inc., Warner Bros. Inc., and Walt Disney Productions.

Thanks also to The Bettman Archive, Inc., Cinemabilia, Culver Pictures, Inc., Foto Fantasies, The Memory Shop, Movie Star Material, Movie Star News, Movie Still Archives, The Penguin Collection, Springer/Bettmann Film Archive, Twentieth Century Antiques, and Van Chromes Corporation.

—D.D.

Additional Filmographies

Mary Pickford's 1909–1917 Films

The Violin Maker of Cremona, 1909
The Lonely Villa, 1909
The Son's Return, 1909
Faded Lilies, 1909
Her First Biscuits, 1909
The Mexican Sweethearts, 1909
The Peach-Basket Hat, 1909
The Way of Man, 1909
The Necklace, 1909
The Country Doctor, 1909
The Cardinal's Conspiracy, 1909
The Renunciation, 1909
Sweet and Twenty, 1909
The Slave, 1909
A Strange Meeting, 1909
They Would Elope, 1909
His Wife's Visitor, 1909
The Indian Runner's Romance, 1909
Oh, Uncle!, 1909
The Seventh Day, 1909
The Little Darling, 1909
The Sealed Room, 1909
1776 (The Hessian Renegades), 1909
Getting Even, 1909
The Broken Locket, 1909
In Old Kentucky, 1909
The Awakening, 1909
The Little Teacher, 1909
His Lost Love, 1909
In the Watches of the Night, 1909
What's Your Hurry?, 1909
The Gibson Goddess, 1909
The Restoration, 1909
The Light That Came, 1909
A Midnight Adventure, 1909
The Mountaineer's Honor, 1909
The Trick That Failed, 1909
The Test, 1909
To Save Her Soul, 1909
All on Account of the Milk, 1910
The Woman from Mellon's, 1910
The Englishman and the Girl, 1910
The Newlyweds, 1910
The Thread of Destiny, 1910
The Twisted Trail, 1910
The Smoker, 1910
As It Is In Life, 1910
A Rich Revenge, 1910
A Romance of the Western Hills, 1910
The Unchanging Sea, 1910
Love Among the Roses, 1910
The Two Brothers, 1910
Ramona, 1910
In the Season of Buds, 1910
A Victim of Jealousy, 1910
A Child's Impulse, 1910

May and December, 1910
Muggsy's First Sweetheart, 1910
Never Again!, 1910
What the Daisy Said, 1910
The Call to Arms, 1910
An Arcadian Maid, 1910
When We Were In Our Teens, 1910
The Sorrows of the
     Unfaithful, 1910
Wilful Peggy, 1910
Muggsy Becomes a Hero, 1910
Examination Day at School, 1910
A Gold Necklace, 1910
The Masher, 1910
A Lucky Toothache, 1910
Waiter Number Five, 1910
Simple Charity, 1910
Song of the Wildwood Flute, 1910
A Plain Song, 1910
White Roses, 1910
When a Man Loves, 1911
The Italian Barber, 1911
Three Sisters, 1911
A Decree of Destiny, 1911
Their First Misunderstanding, 1911
The Dream, 1911
Maid or Man, 1911
At the Duke's Command, 1911
The Mirror, 1911
While the Cat's Away, 1911
Her Darkest Hour, 1911
Artful Kate, 1911
A Manly Man, 1911
The Message in the Bottle, 1911
The Fisher-maid, 1911
In Old Madrid, 1911
Sweet Memories of Yesterday, 1911
The Stampede, 1911
Second Sight, 1911
The Fair Dentist, 1911
For Her Brother's Sake, 1911
The Master and the Man, 1911
The Lighthouse Keeper, 1911
Back to the Soil, 1911
In the Sultan's Garden, 1911
For the Queen's Honor, 1911
A Gasoline Engagement, 1911
At a Quarter to Two, 1911
Science, 1911
The Skating Bug, 1911
The Call of the Song, 1911
The Toss of a Coin, 1911
'Tween Two Loves, 1911
The Rose's Story, 1911
The Sentinel Asleep, 1911
The Better Way, 1911
His Dress Shirt, 1911
From the Bottom of the Sea, 1911

The Courting of Mary, 1911
Love Heeds Not the Showers, 1911
Little Red Riding Hood, 1911
The Caddy's Dream, 1911
Honor Thy Father, 1912
The Mender of Nets, 1912
Iola's Promise, 1912
Fate's Interception, 1912
The Female of the Species, 1912
Just Like a Woman, 1912
Won by a Fish, 1912
The Old Actor, 1912
A Lodging for the Night, 1912
A Beast at Bay, 1912
Home Folks, 1912
Lena and the Geese, 1912
The Schoolteacher and the Wolf, 1912
An Indian Summer, 1912
The Narrow Road, 1912
The Inner Circle, 1912
With the Enemy's Help, 1912
A Pueblo Legend, 1912
Friends, 1912
So Near, Yet So Far, 1912
A Feud in the Kentucky Hills, 1912
The One She Loved, 1912
My Baby, 1912
The Informer, 1912
The Unwelcome Guest, 1912
The New York Hat, 1912
In the Bishop's Carriage, 1913
Caprice, 1913
Hearts Adrift, 1914
A Good Little Devil, 1914
Tess of the Storm Country, 1914
The Eagle's Mate, 1914
Such a Little Queen, 1914
Behind the Scenes, 1914
Cinderella, 1914
Mistress Nell, 1915
Fanchon, The Cricket, 1915
The Dawn of Tomorrow, 1915
Little Pal, 1915
Rags, 1915
Esmeralda, 1915
A Girl of Yesterday, 1915
Madame Butterfly, 1915
The Foundling, 1916
Poor Little Peppina, 1916
The Eternal Grind, 1916
Hulda from Holland, 1916
Less Than the Dust, 1916
The Pride of the Clan, 1917
The Poor Little Rich Girl, 1917
A Romance of the Redwoods, 1917
The Little American, 1917
Rebecca of Sunnybrook Farm, 1917
The Little Princess, 1917

Charlie Chaplin's 1914 Films
Making a Living, 1914
Kid Auto Races at Venice, 1914
Mabel's Strange Predicament, 1914
Between Showers, 1914
A Film Johnnie, 1914
Tango Tangles, 1914
His Favorite Pastime, 1914
Cruel, Cruel Love, 1914
The Star Boarder, 1914
Mabel at the Wheel, 1914
Twenty Minutes of Love, 1914
Caught in a Cabaret, 1914
Caught in the Rain, 1914
A Busy Day, 1914
The Fatal Mallet, 1914
Her Friend the Bandit, 1914
The Knockout, 1914
Mabel's Busy Day, 1914
Mabel's Married Life, 1914
Laughing Gas, 1914
The Property Man, 1914
The Face on the Bar-room Floor, 1914
Recreation, 1914
The Masquerader, 1914
His New Profession, 1914
The Rounders, 1914
The New Janitor, 1914
Those Love Pangs, 1914
Dough and Dynamite, 1914
Gentlemen of Nerve, 1914
His Musical Career, 1914
His Trysting Place, 1914
Tillie's Punctured Romance, 1914
Getting Acquainted, 1914
His Prehistoric Past, 1914

Marlene Dietrich's 1923–1929 Films
The Little Napoleon, 1923
Tragedy of Love, 1923
Man by the Roadside, 1923
The Leap Into Life, 1924
The Joyless Street, 1925
Manon Lescaut, 1926
A Modern Du Barry, 1926
Heads Up, Charly!, 1926
Madame Wants No Children, 1926
The Imaginary Baron, 1927
His Greatest Bluff, 1927
Cafe Electric, 1927
The Art of Love, 1928
I Kiss Your Hand, Madame, 1929
Three Loves, 1929
The Ship of Lost Men, 1929
Dangers of the Engagement Period, 1929

Selected Bibliography

Mary Pickford

Pickford, Mary. *Sunshine and Shadow*. Garden City, N.Y.: Doubleday, 1955.

Windeler, Robert. *Sweetheart: The Story of Mary Pickford*. New York: Praeger, 1974.

Charlie Chaplin

Chaplin, Charles. *My Autobiography*. New York: Simon and Schuster, 1964.

McCabe, John. *Charlie Chaplin*. Garden City, N.Y.: Doubleday, 1978.

Gloria Swanson

Swanson, Gloria. *Swanson on Swanson*. New York: Random House, 1980.

Rudolph Valentino

Walker, Alexander. *Rudolph Valentino*. New York: Stein and Day, 1976.

Greta Garbo

Sands, Frederick, and Broman, Sven. *The Divine Garbo*. New York: Grosset and Dunlap, 1979.

Clark Gable

Tornabene, Lyn. *Long Live the King*. New York: Putnam, 1976.

Marlene Dietrich

Higham, Charles. *Marlene: The Life of Marlene Dietrich*. New York: Norton, 1977.

Errol Flynn

Flynn, Errol. *My Wicked, Wicked Ways*. New York: Buccaneer Books, 1959.

Freedland, Michael. *The Two Lives of Errol Flynn*. New York: Morrow, 1978.

Mae West

Eells, George, and Musgrove, Stanley. *Mae West*. New York: Morrow, 1982.

W. C. Fields

Taylor, Robert Lewis. *W. C. Fields: His Follies and Fortunes*. Garden City, N.Y.: Doubleday, 1949.

Astaire and Rogers

Croce, Arlene. *The Fred Astaire and Ginger Rogers Book*. New York: Outerbridge and Lazard, 1972.

Fred Astaire

Astaire, Fred. *Steps in Time*. New York: Da Capo Press, 1959.

Green, Benny. *Fred Astaire*. New York: Exeter Books, 1979.

The Marx Brothers

Adamson, Joe. *Groucho, Harpo, Chico and Sometimes Zeppo*. New York: Simon and Schuster, 1973.

Joan Crawford

Newquist, Roy. *Conversations with Joan Crawford*. Secaucus, N.J.: Citadel Press, 1968.

Humphrey Bogart

Benchley, Nathaniel. *Humphrey Bogart*. Boston: Little, Brown, 1975.

Bette Davis

Davis, Bette. *The Lonely Life*. New York: Putnam, 1962.

Cary Grant

Guthrie, Lee. *The Life and Loves of Cary Grant*. New York: Drake Publishers, 1977.

Katharine Hepburn

Higham, Charles. *Kate: The Life of Katharine Hepburn*. New York: Norton, 1975.

Judy Garland

Frank, Gerold. *Judy*. New York: Harper and Row, 1975.

John Wayne

Eyles, Allen. *John Wayne*. South Brunswick, N.J.: A. S. Barnes, 1979.

Elizabeth Taylor

Hirsch, Foster. *Elizabeth Taylor*. New York: Galahad Books, 1973.

James Dean

Herndon, Venable. *James Dean: A Short Life*. Garden City, N.Y.: Doubleday, 1974.

Marilyn Monroe

Guiles, Fred Lawrence. *Norma Jean: The Life of Marilyn Monroe*. New York: McGraw-Hill, 1969.

Mailer, Norman. *Marilyn: A Biography*. New York: Grosset and Dunlap, 1973.

Barbra Streisand

Spada, James, with Nickens, Christopher. *Barbra Streisand: The Woman and the Legend*. Garden City, N.Y.: Doubleday, 1981.

Robert Redford

Reed, Donald A. *Robert Redford: A Photographic Portrait of the Man and His Films*. New York: Popular Library, 1975.

Jane Fonda

Guiles, Fred Lawrence. *Jane Fonda: The Actress in Her Time*. Garden City, N.Y.: Doubleday, 1982.

Warren Beatty

Quirk, Lawrence J. *The Films of Warren Beatty*. Secaucus, N.J.: Citadel Press, 1981.

Jack Nicholson

Crane, Robert David, and Fryer, Christopher. *Jack Nicholson: Face to Face*. New York: M. Evans and Company, 1975.

Diane Keaton

Munshower, Suzanne. *The Diane Keaton Scrapbook*. New York: Grosset and Dunlap, 1979.

Woody Allen

Yacowar, Maurice. *Loser Take All: The Comic Art of Woody Allen*. New York: Frederick Ungar, 1979.

Burt Reynolds

Streebeck, Nancy. *The Films of Burt Reynolds*. Secaucus, N.J.: Citadel Press, 1982.

George Lucas

Arnold, Alan. *Once Upon a Galaxy: A Journal of the Making of The Empire Strikes Back*. New York: Ballantine, 1980.

Steven Spielberg

Kotzwinkle, William. *E.T. The Extraterrestrial Scrapbook*. New York: Putnam, 1982.

Reference Books and Miscellaneous

Gertner, Richard, ed. *International Motion Picture Almanac 1982*. New York: Quigley Publishing Co., Inc., 1982.

Griffith, Richard; Mayer, Arthur, and Bowser, Eileen. *The Movies*. New York: Simon and Schuster, 1981.

Katz, Ephraim. *The Film Encyclopedia*. New York: Crowell, 1979.

Michael, Paul, ed. *The American Movies Reference Book: The Sound Era*. Englewood Cliffs, N.J.: Prentice-Hall, 1969.

Walker, Alexander. *Stardom: A Hollywood Phenomenon*. New York: Stein and Day, 1970.

Film Copyrights and Photography Credits

Index

OVERLEAF: In the closing scene of *The Empire Strikes Back*, C-3PO, R2-D2, Luke Skywalker, and Princess Leia in the Rebel Cruiser look out at the Rebel fleet passing before them.

Steven Spielberg's beloved E.T. The Extra-Terrestrial phones home.

The text was set in Futura Book by U.S. Lithograph Inc.,
New York, New York.

The book was printed by Toppan Printing Company, Ltd.,
Tokyo, Japan.